DISCOVERING PUB NAMES AND SIGNS

David Brandon

SHIRE PUBLICATIONS

First published in Great Britain in 2010 by Shire Publications Ltd, Midland House, West Way, Botley, Oxford OX2 0PH, United Kingdom.
44-02 23rd Street, Suite 219, Long Island City, NY 11101, USA.

E-mail: shire@shirebooks.co.uk www.shirebooks.co.uk

A CIP catalogue record for this book is available from the British Library.

Shire Discovering no. 301 • ISBN-978 0 74780 757 5

Designed by Tony Truscott Designs, Henfield, West Sussex, UK and typeset in Garamond.
Printed in China through Worldprint.

10 11 12 13 14 10 9 8 7 6 5 4 3 2 1

ACKNOWLEDGEMENTS

The author would like to thank Linda and Ed Brandon for their practical assistance and the following for generously allowing me to reproduce images in their possession: Brian: Marquis of Granby – Black Bull; Elliott Brown: Great Western; Gordon Cragg: Dun Cow; Mark Dodds: The Angel; Ian D. Harrison: Orange Tree; David Kirkby: Case is Altered; Elissa Motter: Seahorse; Ewan Munro: Cartoonist; L. J. Platt: Shroppie Fly; Alan & Carol Rose: Cat & Custard Pot – Sherlock Holmes; Mike Smith: Duke of Wellington; Thorskegga Thorn: Traveller's Rest; Simon Ward, Divedart: Donkey & Buskins; Susan Watts: cover image – Robin Hood.

Contents

Introduction	4
Religious Signs	8
Transport Signs	12
Royal and Heraldic Signs	16
Horse-racing Signs	20
Nautical Signs	23
Sporting Signs	27
Artistic Signs	30
Railway Signs	34
Fighting Heroes	38
Mammal Signs	42
Birds, Fish and Other Creatures	46
Folklore and Legend	50
Literary Signs	53
Trade and Occupational Signs	56
Food and Drink	59
Some Curious Names and Signs	62
Some Miscellaneous Signs	68
Pub-sign Artists	70
Pubs with Nicknames	74
Further Reading	76
Index	78

Introduction

THE HISTORY of signboards and trade signs goes back at least two thousand years. When most people were illiterate, there was a need for retail premises to display a clearly identifiable pictorial sign indicating and advertising the nature of the business being carried on within. Signs have been in decline for two centuries now, as literacy has increased and become almost universal. The three brass balls of the pawnbroker are still seen quite frequently; occasionally a chemist's shop may display a pestle and mortar or carboys containing coloured water; a barber's shop may show a pole with a symbolic red bandage, and a tailor's premises a pair of shears. One type of trade sign that continues to be familiar is the pub or inn sign.

It is likely that the inhabitants of Britain had discovered the pleasures of alcoholic drinks long before the Romans arrived, although it is not known whether they had any kind of communal place for drinking. The Romans had no liking for drinks based on barley but were great devotees of wine, and the *tabernae* which they introduced to Britain were places where wine could be consumed on the premises or bought and taken away. *Tabernae* (from which we get our word 'tavern') were likely to have been located in the towns that were an important part of Roman culture, and it seems that a garland composed of vine leaves or something looking like a bush was placed outside these buildings to draw attention to the delights available within, especially when there was a new vintage. The common sign the Grapes may reflect this, as does the expression 'A good wine needs no bush'.

Among the various invaders who settled in Britain after the Romans left were the Saxons, who were certainly ale-drinkers. Brewing was seen as women's work and it is likely that people drank ale in the crude hovels in which most of them lived. It may be, however, that some of these women (known as 'brewsters') developed a reputation for consistently good ale and decided to make some money by opening their premises to locals and others and to sell the ale. To advertise the product on offer, an ale-stake would be displayed. This was a wooden pole protruding from the front of the building and decorated with a bunch of greenery. Alternatively, an upright pole close to the building might serve the same purpose. Another distinguishing feature of many drinking places was a lattice arrangement, usually painted red, placed across the windows to let light in but allow some privacy for those inside. Occasionally a pub name recalls this arrangement, such as Lattice House at King's Lynn, Norfolk. Over the years many pub names have become corrupted and one in central London in its last years had the name 'Green Lettuce'.

There are many contenders for the title of oldest pub in Britain. One of these is Ye Olde Trip to Jerusalem at Nottingham, which is claimed to date back to the end of the twelfth century, around the time when names were probably first bestowed on pubs. Although there is no evidence supporting its claim to have been a meeting place for men making their way as crusaders to the Holy Land, it is a wonderful and unique name. In 1393 Richard II ordered all public drinking places to display a prominent sign. This was to assist the ale-taster in what must have been his congenial peripatetic task of quality control. It was important to maintain standards in staple items of diet such as ale and bread. William Shakespeare's father was an ale-taster. A publican whose licence was revoked for such misdemeanours as watering his ale was legally required to remove the sign.

In the bushes or garlands outside the Roman *tabernae* and in the Saxon ale-stakes it seems we have the origins of pub signs. Like most street furniture, it may be the very familiarity of pub signs that means that they are often seen but rarely looked at. This is a paradox because they are, of course, advertisements. Their history has received comparatively little attention from academic historians and some people have disparaged them as being merely popular or people's art. However, some great artists have been paid for painting them, and even today new painters appear to continue the proud tradition of creating exceptional examples of a specialised form of artwork. They still take great care to research their subjects and to portray them accurately.

Pub signs and names provide an intriguing insight into the wonderful diversity that is the history of the United Kingdom, not least into some of its more fascinating and largely forgotten backwaters. Even the signs themselves come in a variety of types. As well as the painted board hanging from a bracket, usually projecting from the front of the building, there are boards atop free-standing poles and boards attached to the walls of the pub. There are 'gallows signs' hanging from a structure supported by uprights on both sides of the street; there are signs painted on gable ends, signs composed of glazed tiles, signs carved in stone; there are three-dimensional signs, including at least one made of topiary, and a living sign consisting of a fully active beehive. Some signs are 'double-headers', which have different but related images on each side.

From time to time, but especially in Tudor days, there have been attempts to make signs more conspicuous, but none has ever equalled the monstrous erection at the White Hart at Scole in Norfolk. This spanned the road and displayed twenty-five life-sized figures. It was said to have cost £1,000 – a king's ransom when it was put up in 1655. The gallows signs, which spanned the road, were certainly eye-catching and were quite common before the eighteenth century. In 1718, one in Bride Lane, Fleet Street, collapsed and brought down the front wall of the building supporting it. Four passers-by were crushed to death. The law decreed that no new gallows signs were to be erected but a few survive, including those at the George, Stamford, Lincolnshire, and Ye Old Starre, York.

This book is intended to provide a brief introduction to the stories behind a selection of signs and names, with emphasis on the strange and quirky. Generally the names examined are unusual, are not what they might seem to be at first, or provide a good story – an insight into a quirky element of history. The three most common pub names are Royal Oak, Red Lion and Rose and Crown. Other very common names include Angel, Bell, Coach and Horses, Cross Keys, George and Dragon, King's Head, (Lord) Nelson, Plough, Swan, Wheatsheaf and White Hart. Many other signs are variations or derivatives of these.

Pubs and their attendant signs are disappearing at a depressingly rapid rate. Pub names are also changing, the new ones rarely being an improvement. Many of the pub-owning companies display little interest in advertising their houses with eye-catching signs, and the names they bestow on some of them are either bland, banal or sometimes simply meaningless, showing no sense of history whatever. Where it is known that an establishment has closed or changed its name, this will be indicated in this book but complete accuracy cannot be guaranteed, given the speed of change in the hospitality industry. The author is aware that there are technical or semantic differences between pubs, inns, bars, hotels, taps, taverns, etc, but for the sake of simplicity they are all included here under the generic term 'pubs'.

Describing the derivation of pub names is not an exact science. The origins of many names are disputed or sometimes simply unknown. In the main body of the book, names are arranged around themes. This is a compromise for the sake of convenience, because not everything is what it appears to be in the world of pub signs and names. What one expert claims to be a sign of religious origin, for example, will for another be a sign related to a trade. Only when the name of a pub is thought to be unique, or there is something else special about it, will its location be mentioned. For the sake of brevity, the indefinite article is omitted before the names of pubs.

Religious Signs

A GREAT many names are of religious or biblical origin. This reflects the major role played by religion in medieval society. Furthermore, the provision of accommodation and hospitality for travellers was seen as a Christian duty and many of the monastic orders opened wayside inns for those travelling around on business or making their way as pilgrims to places associated with miracles and holy relics.

Angel. In biblical terms an angel is a being intermediate between God and man. Among other functions, they sing and play musical instruments, carry important messages and make announcements. The way they are visualised blowing horns and having wings and flowing robes provides ample opportunity for fanciful depiction on signboards. Variations include Angel and Elephant (Widnes, Cheshire), Angel and Greyhound (Oxford) and Angel and White Horse (Tadcaster, North Yorkshire).

Bull. This pub name often refers to the animal, which would have been very familiar in what was once a rural and agricultural society, but on occasions it refers to a 'papal bull', a formal and important document issued by a Pope. A sign at Market Deeping, Lincolnshire, showed the animal on one side and a papal bull concerning the nearby Crowland Abbey on the other.

Catherine Wheel. Every child loves the firework of this name. Few realise that Catherine was a young Christian woman martyred on a wheel for her faith. The wheel was adopted as the badge of the Knights of St Catherine of Sinai, a military order who guarded pilgrims travelling to holy places. Perhaps some of the pilgrims' hostels were given this name. A variation is St Catherine Wheel, Hereford. The Catherine Wheel also appears on the arms of the Worshipful Company of Turners.

Christopher. This rare sign refers to St Christopher, the patron saint of travellers. It was believed that if someone setting out on a journey gazed on an image of St Christopher before departure their safety would be guaranteed for the day. In medieval times our ancestors would often make a quick visit to the local church, where an image of St Christopher was frequently painted on the north wall opposite the main doorway, which was usually on the south side. Traces of such mural paintings can still be seen in some old churches. Nowadays, of course, some people carry a St Christopher medallion as they travel. Examples with this name can be found at Bath and Eton.

Cock and Pye. This unusual sign commemorated a blasphemous late-medieval oath referring to the Cross and the Pyx.

Cross Keys. This very common sign refers to St Peter, who was entrusted by Jesus with the keys to heaven. To be heraldically correct, one key should be silver, the other gold. The Cross Keys at York is in the city centre, close to York Minster, which is dedicated to St Peter. The Cross Keys at Dolgellau, Gwynedd, has an attractive bilingual sign tucked away off the main street of this small North Wales town.

The Old Crutched Friar, London EC3. 'Crutched' derives from 'crossed' and refers to the Friars of the Holy Cross, who had their headquarters in the vicinity. They wore a prominent red cross on their habits. At one time the sign showed two friars hobbling about on crutches. Whether this humour was intentional or unintentional is not known.

Today the sign has lost the 'old' and is attractive, although it is not clear whether the artist knows the significance of 'crutched'.

George and Dragon. This common sign allows the painter to exercise imagination in depicting the dragon. Some very exotic beasts can be seen. St George became the patron saint of England when he was imposed on the country by the Normans, though the Saxon people regarded Edward the Confessor as their patron saint. The battle between George and the dragon is an allegory of good overcoming evil.

George and Pilgrims, Glastonbury, Somerset. This impressive ancient building started as a hostelry for pilgrims to the local abbey and became a secular inn when the abbey was dissolved.

Golden Cross is a fairly unusual sign. At Coventry, this name is thought by some to have been given to the pub because there was once a mint producing gold coins on the site where it now stands.

Hope and Anchor appears at first to be a juxtaposition of two very different elements. In biblical terms, however, the anchor is the symbol of salvation and hope.

Lamb and Flag. This fairly common sign usually depicts the *Agnus Dei*, the Lamb of God. This is a symbol of Christ's Passion. It frequently shows the lamb complete with a cross, a halo and a banner of victory, the banner being placed between the animal's forefeet. The well-known hostelry with this name in Covent Garden, London, is also known as the 'Bucket of Blood' because prizefighting used to take place on the premises.

St John's Head. A very rare sign, this depicts the gory biblical story in which Salome entranced King Herod with her voluptuous gyrations as she danced in front of him. Allowing lust to rule his brain, Herod promised Salome anything she wanted. After some thought, she requested the head of John the Baptist. Herod was rather disconcerted by this unexpected request but dared not renege on his promise, and so John was beheaded and his head was presented on a salver. The Jerusalem Tavern, London EC1, shows John's severed head on a plate. A variation is St Edmund's Head, Bury St Edmunds, Suffolk. Edmund died for his faith but was either scourged, shot with arrows and beheaded or broken on the wheel.

Salutation. A familiar sign, this refers to the Annunciation, when the Archangel Gabriel greeted the Virgin Mary and informed her of the Incarnation. It can double up as a greeting, a friendly gesture between friends or equally from the publican to his guests.

Saracen's Head. The Crusades were theoretically a religious war. Signs with this name nearly always depict the enemy as fearsome and cruel-looking.

Seven Stars. This common name alludes to the seven stars supposedly around the halo of the Virgin Mary. Contrarily, the Seven Stars at Derby depicts a vessel sailing at night with the seven stars visible in the sky.

Three Kings. Three has been described as the perfect number, expressing the beginning, the middle and the end, and therefore often used as a symbol of deity. This particular sign usually refers to the Magi, who supposedly were the three wise men from the East who brought gifts to the infant Jesus at Bethlehem shortly after his birth. The number three has a mystical significance in many cultures and religions and there are numerous pub signs that include this number. Other examples that may have religious origins are Three Boars (Wymondham, Norfolk), Three Goat's Heads (Oxford), referring to St Anthony, and Three Swans (Market Harborough, Leicestershire) referring to St Hugh. The pub at Market Harborough has a particularly fine wrought-iron sign.

Transport Signs

TRANSPORT and communication are the lifeblood of advanced societies. In pre-industrial Britain, the best means of travel and transport was by water. In the eighteenth and nineteenth centuries, radical improvements in road engineering and the building of canals and later railways effected a revolution in the speed and efficiency with which raw materials, manufactured goods, people and ideas could be moved around. Many pub signs celebrate the crucial role played by transport in British history.

Coach and Horses. Some fine signs depict the stagecoaches that provided a comprehensive system of internal passenger transport before the advent of the railways from the 1830s. Although usually given a romantic spin, coach travel was actually expensive, uncomfortable and hazardous. Some signs commemorate the names of individual coaches. Examples are Dairy Maid (Aylesbury, Buckinghamshire) and Perseverance (Havant, Hampshire). These can be puzzling if the observer does not know that our ancestors were in the habit of giving stagecoaches such names.

Drovers' Arms. Pubs with this name tend to be found beside the routes along which livestock was driven, mostly from the upland parts of northern England and of Wales, to the rich pastureland close to London, where the animals were fattened up before being taken to markets such as Smithfield to be butchered and sold.

Guide over Sands, Allithwaite, Cumbria. Allithwaite is a hamlet overlooking Morecambe Bay. It is at the northern end of a highly hazardous footpath that can be taken at low tide under certain conditions across the shifting sands. The sign shows Cedric Robinson, who has been the 'Queen's Guide to the Sands' for over forty-five years. The walk across the bay must not be undertaken without guidance.

Hackney Cab, London E8. This unusual, possibly unique sign plays on the name of the locality but depicts what should correctly be called a hackney *carriage*. A 'hackney' was a high-stepping harness horse.

Hansom Cab, York. Joseph Aloysius Hansom (1803–82) was born in York. He was an architect of national repute who designed, among other buildings, Birmingham Town Hall and the Roman Catholic Cathedral at Plymouth. Perhaps ironically, he is best-known for the 'Patent Safety (Hansom) Cab which first saw the light of day in 1834 and which went on to become such a familiar item on the streets of Britain's Victorian cities, most especially London.

Lock, Stock and Barrel, Newbury, Berkshire. Close to the Kennet & Avon Canal, this pub has a fine sign showing a narrowboat in a canal lock with the gates being closed behind it. The boat has an impressive stock of barrels on board. It cleverly puns on the firearms term, 'lock, stock, and barrel', indicating the completeness of something by the presence of all its parts.

Midget. This unique sign adorns a pub at Abingdon in Oxfordshire, where the MG factory was located from 1929 to 1980, the company then being the largest employer in the town. Most of the cars produced were rather small and many were decidedly sporty, including the MG Midget. The pub was originally called The Magic Midget after a record-breaking MG of the 1930s.

Navigation. Canals and other artificial waterways used to be referred to as 'navigations'. Most of the pubs with this name were originally built to provide refreshment for thirsty navvies engaged in building the canals or to serve the men and women who worked the barges and other vessels on what were vital transport arteries for industry and agriculture.

Packhorse. The woollen industry was a source of great wealth for Britain before the Industrial Revolution. Fleeces were bulky but light and the best means of moving them across the country was in trains of mules and horses which could pick their way around

the muddy morasses or dust-bowls which passed for roads during much of the year.

Packhorse and Talbot, Chiswick, London W4. This unique sign with its juxtaposition of subjects is probably the result of the amalgamation of two former pubs. The design of the sign itself is unusual.

Running Footman, Mayfair, London. Travel by carriage was slow before eighteenth-century road improvements. Wealthy families employed young men called 'running footmen' to jog along in front of their carriages, paying tolls and warning innkeepers that prestigious customers were on their way. They wore their master's livery. The full name of this pub is 'I Am the Only Running Footman'.

Scotsman's Pack, Hathersage, Derbyshire. This sign remembers the Scottish pedlars who used to travel down into England hawking various distinctive items made in Scotland and not normally easy to get hold of elsewhere. A favourite item was tough and warm tweed material. Trudging through the countryside was thirsty work and it may be that the Scotsman was a welcome customer in the inn because he would have several drinks before setting off on the road once more.

Shroppie Fly. This uniquely named house near Crewe on the Shropshire Union Canal refers to 'fly boats'. These were express boats that operated to a tight timetable, were drawn by relays of frequently changed horses, had priority over all other canal traffic and were used to convey perishable merchandise and passengers who were in a hurry.

Tollgate. This fairly rare sign recalls the turnpike road system, which expanded rapidly in the eighteenth century. Trustees were given the legal right to enclose specified stretches of road. The tolls they levied from the users were for the purpose of maintaining the road in satisfactory condition. Gates were erected across the road, being opened to users on payment of the requisite toll. Most of the tollgates have gone but many tollhouses remain as private dwellings and their shape often gives their previous purpose away. The Turnpike pub in Yarnton, Oxfordshire, shows a rather jovial-looking pike doing a rapid body swerve.

Tramways, Southampton. The electric tramway systems that operated in many British towns and cities from the early twentieth century until after the Second World War generated considerable affection and feelings of nostalgia among those old enough to remember them, even if the memories are viewed through rose-tinted glasses. Many of the tram systems were highly individualistic and undoubtedly added character to their surroundings. The sign for this pub shows a Southampton Corporation open-top tram passing through the city's well-known medieval Bargate. There were also closed-top trams on the system and these had an unusual domed roof profile so that they could negotiate the Bargate. The Bargate was bypassed in the 1930s and the last trams in Southampton ran on the final day of 1949.

Travellers Rest. The name brings to mind a weary and footsore traveller breaking his journey to enjoy a good sit-down followed by refreshment and hospitality in congenial surroundings.

Waggon and Horses. Before the coming of the canals and then the railways, bulky and heavy goods were transported in horse-drawn waggons. These moved ponderously and often became stuck in the ruts or foundered in the potholes that were a feature of the roads before improved road surfaces were developed from the seventeenth century. Wayside inns offered refreshment for thirsty waggoners. The Waggon and Horses at Thrupp, Gloucestershire, hosts meetings of the Ducati Monster Motorcycle Club and the artist has depicted the old slow form of cartage above a fine example of a Ducati.

Royal and Heraldic Signs

MEDIEVAL SOCIETY was dominated by the Crown, the Church and the land-owning barons, and their influences are very evident in pub signs and names. Portraits of monarchs and other grandees are common, but sometimes, especially in the case of royalty, the reference takes the form of a symbol extracted from their armorial bearings and the origin may not be obvious. Complete armorial bearings of monarchs, other royalty and the great landed families are common, but there are also many signs depicting the arms of various craft guilds and those of many towns and cities.

Alexandra Vaults, Saltburn-by-the-Sea, North Yorkshire. The sign depicts Queen Alexandra, the long-suffering wife of the playboy King Edward VII.

Anne of Cleves, Broxbourne, Hertfordshire, and Melton Mowbray, Leicestershire. Anne was Henry VIII's fourth wife. Henry had not seen Anne before she arrived in England on 1 January 1540 to marry him. When the King met her, he was horrified with what he saw and disparagingly referred to her as the 'Flanders Mare'. The marriage took place but was never consummated and quickly annulled.

Bear and Billet, Bear and Ragged Staff, and variations. A handful of pubs display one or other of these signs, which are derived from the badge of the fifteenth-century Richard Neville, Earl of Warwick, who exercised such power that he was nicknamed 'the Kingmaker'. Some of them, however, may recall the 'sport' of bear-baiting, in which a large and ferocious bear was chained to a strong wooden post and had dogs set on it.

Blue Boar. A wild and ferocious-looking blue boar usually refers to the heraldic device of the Earls of Oxford, one of whom was on the winning Lancastrian side at the decisive Battle of Bosworth (1485), which ended the Wars of the Roses.

Cavendish Arms, Cartmel, Cumbria. This attractive heraldic sign shows that the family of the Dukes of Devonshire owned land in the area.

Cordwainers' Arms. This uncommon sign is taken from the arms of the Worshipful Company of that name. They received their charter in 1439. Cordwainers originally worked with goatskin leather from Spain. Three Goats' Heads, an unusual sign, also refers to the Company of Cordwainers.

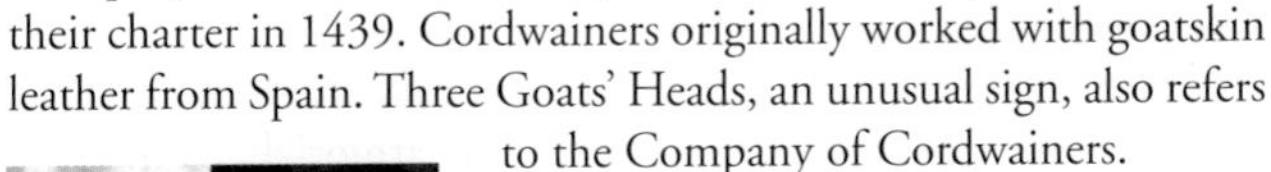

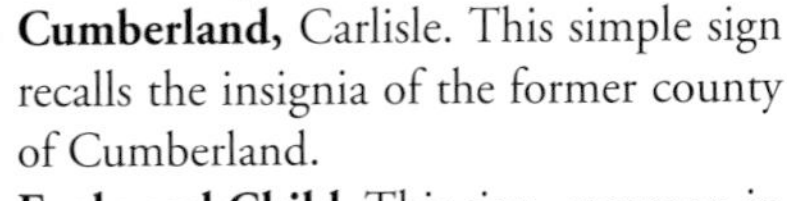

Cumberland, Carlisle. This simple sign recalls the insignia of the former county of Cumberland.

Eagle and Child. This sign, common in the north-west of England, refers to a legend concerning the powerful Stanley family, who owned large tracts of land there and in the Isle of Man.

Fitzwilliam Arms. This is just one example of the many signs commemorating a major land-owning family. Pubs with this name could be found in South Yorkshire and near Peterborough. That at Marholm, just outside Peterborough, has a very fine topiary sign which has led to the pub being known locally as the 'Green Man'.

Four Marys, Linlithgow, West Lothian, Scotland. The ill-fated Mary, Queen of Scots, was born at Linlithgow Palace on 8 December 1542 and her troubles started six days later when her father died and she became queen. This pub celebrates her faithful servants, all called Mary, respectively Hamilton, Seaton, Beaton and Livingston.

Golden Lion. This popular heraldic sign is usually taken as referring to Henry I (reigned 1100–35).

King's Head. Many different kings appear on pub signs. This one at Southwold in Suffolk depicts Henry VII (reigned 1485–1509). His claim to the throne was tenuous, but in his case might was right.

Oakeley Arms, Maentwrog, Gwynedd. This fine heraldic sign shows the arms of a family who made a fortune from owning slate mines in the district.

Princess of Wales. The example of this sign in Bristol depicts Diana, the Princess of Wales who died tragically in 1997. Even before she married Prince Charles, one or two pubs commemorated her on their signs but after her marriage the usual official embargo on portraying living members of the royal family came into effect. Only after her untimely death could signs like the one at Bristol be displayed.

Red Lion, Southwold, Suffolk. This is an unusual but simple version of a very common sign relating to John of Gaunt, Duke of Lancaster (1340–99), the fourth son of Edward III.

Rising Sun. This is a common sign associated with the armorial bearings of Edward III (reigned 1327–77) and Richard III. After Edward's wife, Philippa of Hainault, died, he took up with a rapacious mistress, Alice Perrers, many years his junior, who was extremely unpopular and described by a courtier as 'that wanton baggage'. She and her daughter were in the habit of sleeping with the King together and infected him with a sexually-transmitted disease.

Royal Oak. One of the commonest signs, this usually shows a spreading oak, often with a cameo in the foliage depicting the head of Charles II. The sign became popular after the Restoration of Charles in 1660 and it commemorates the tree at Boscobel in

Shropshire in which he is said to have hidden from his Parliamentary pursuers after his defeat at the Battle of Worcester in 1651. At Banks in Lancashire a rare version of this sign depicts the whole of Charles II's armorial bearing in the tree.

Slubbers' Arms. This very rare sign remembers the textile workers known as 'slubbers' who worked with wool or cotton fibre, preparing it for the spinning process. Perhaps the slubbers slaked their thirsts in one particular pub, which became associated with them and their trade.

Talbot. This large, white and magnificent breed of dog, now extinct, was kept for hunting in medieval times. The sign relates to the badge of the powerful Talbot family, the Earls of Shrewsbury.

Unicorn. This fairly common sign depicts the mythical single-horned horse-like creature. Among the tales about this fabulous beast was the belief that its horn in powdered form was a powerful aphrodisiac. Its appearance on pub signs, however, is more likely to derive from the English royal arms, whose supporters are a lion and a unicorn. A unicorn also appears on the arms of three livery companies, the Goldsmiths, the Wax Chandlers and the Apothecaries.

Victoria. Victoria is one of the monarchs most often commemorated in pub names. After she was widowed, she became reclusive and so unpopular that a strong republican movement developed.

White Horse. This very popular sign was a device on the battle standards of the Saxons, the badge of Kent, an item on the coats of arms of several livery companies such as the Farriers and the Wheelwrights, and was also associated with the Hanoverian dynasty of British monarchs in the eighteenth and nineteenth centuries. At least one sign depicts a 'white horse' such as those carved through the turf on chalk hillsides.

White Lion. This common sign is associated with Edward IV (reigned 1461–70 and 1471–83). A tall, well-built, charming man, possessed of a prodigious sex drive, he was a leading figure on the Yorkist side in the Wars of the Roses. He is thought to have died of pneumonia.

Horse-racing Signs

THE FIRST recorded race meeting in Britain seems to have been held at Smithfield in London in 1174. Horse-racing became popular when Queen Anne (reigned 1702–14) became almost obsessed with it. The Jockey Club regulated and codified horse-racing in 1752, since when it has developed into a major industry, the governing body of which is now the British Horseracing Board. A number of pub signs reflect the development of horse-racing and they include some that are unique because they refer to specific horses, often bred and trained in the locality of the pub concerned. Casual passers-by may be puzzled by such signs, which usually show a thoroughbred horse and a name that seems to have no connection with anything equine.

Alice Hawthorne, Wheldrake, near York. This is an example of a sign that does not obviously appear to refer to a horse. But Alice Hawthorne was quite a horse. Bred locally and supposedly named after the owner's mistress, she was raced seventy-one times in the mid-1840s and won fifty-one of those races.

Altisidora, Bishop Burton, East Yorkshire. A local landowner had every reason to be grateful to the horse of this name in 1813 when he staked every last penny he had on Altisidora, which romped home in the St Leger. He renamed the local pub, which he owned, in honour of the animal.

Brigadier Gerard, York. Named after the hero of a series of stories by Arthur Conan Doyle, Brigadier Gerard was a very successful horse which retired from racing in 1973.

Cadland, Chilwell, Notts. The name of this old pub is a reference to a horse which won the Derby in 1828 and went on to win the £2,000 Guineas in the same year.

Charles XII, Heslington, York. The sign commemorates a horse owned by a member of the local gentry. Charles XII had an extremely successful career, winning the St Leger in 1839 and the Gold Cup two days later, after apparently having been walked from York to take part in these races at Doncaster. He is said to have won sixty more races during a racing life of almost ten years. He was put down in 1859.

Flying Childers. This extremely rare sign recalls a very successful racehorse of the mid-eighteenth century. It was owned by the fourth Duke of Devonshire and apparently won prize money of around £20,000.

Flying Dutchman. A horse of this name won the Derby in 1849 and is commemorated on at least one sign. Sometimes the sign shows the legendary spectral ship, which is supposedly condemned forever to haunt the seas around the Cape of Good Hope, bringing ill luck to all who see it.

Horse and Jockey, Horse and Groom. Signs with obvious equine associations such as these are often, although not necessarily, found in places associated with the 'sport of kings'.

Master Robert, Heston, Middlesex. The subject of the sign at this pub on the old Great West Road is a horse which, remarkably, graduated from pulling a plough and later a milk cart to winning the Grand National. The original sign was a masterpiece painted by Lynwood Palmer, whose paintings of racehorses were bought by the richest patrons of the turf and made him a personal fortune.

Racecourse. An uncommon sign, this pub at Whittington Moor, Chesterfield, was close to the site of a former racecourse. Nearby is another possibly unique sign, Donkey Derby, which also commemorates the racing that used to take place there.

St Leger. This unusual sign recalls the classic race of that name which takes place every year at Doncaster and was run for the first time in 1776.

Spinner and Bergamot, Comberbach, Cheshire. This puzzling sign showed the heads of two racehorses. The pub was originally called 'Spinner' after the local textile industry. A local landowner who frequented the pub liked it so much that he named a racehorse after it. It went on to win several races for him, as did a later horse, Bergamot. They make a charming combination.

Stable Door. This unusual sign is most often found in places where racehorses are trained. One example could be found at Middleham in North Yorkshire, where such horses are an everyday sight in the lanes around the village.

Starting Gate. This uncommon sign is occasionally found near racecourses. An associated and equally unusual name is Winning Post.

Tattersall's Tavern, London SW7. Tattersall's is a London auction house, founded in 1766 and specialising in sales of bloodstock. The eponymous Tattersall played a leading role looking after the wealthy Duke of Kingston's stud.

Why Not?, Sheffield. The horse with this name won the Grand National in 1894. The licensee of the pub at the time placed a bet on it and came away a considerably richer man. He was so grateful that he renamed the pub in the horse's honour. A handful of other pubs have the same name, perhaps celebrating this splendid animal. However, one at Andover, Hampshire, was supposed to have gained this name because for years a brewery kept applying to the local authority for permission to build a new pub. Time and time again the request was refused but when the pub did eventually open and gain its licence it was given this ironic name as a swipe at the council.

Nautical Signs

THE BRITISH ISLES possess a long coastline but because they are small nowhere is very far from the coast. For this reason the presence of the sea has had a major influence on innumerable aspects of Britain's economic, political, social and cultural history and this is reflected in large numbers of pub signs and names with a nautical or maritime link, even in places some distance inland.

Aleppo Merchant, Carno, Powys, Wales. It is thought that this pub gained its curious name because a former licensee had an ancestor who owned or worked on a ship of this name which traded with what used to be known as the Levant. This was the eastern seaboard of the Mediterranean, now comprising Lebanon, Syria and Israel.

Ark Royal. This uncommon sign commemorates several generations of fighting ships with this name. In the twentieth century it came to be associated with a number of Royal Navy aircraft carriers.

Bell, Walberswick, Suffolk. Signs for pubs with this name most often refer to church bells, or occasionally to hand bells, so this one, which shows a ship's bell, is unusual.

Brass Monkey, Fareham, Hampshire. Contrary to popular perception, a brass monkey was a rack used on the deck of a warship for storing cannonballs in the days of muzzle-loading naval guns. In freezing weather the balls on the brass monkey could get quite cold.

The cannon balls would often fall off the rack because the temperature caused the metal of the brass monkey to shrink.

Endeavour. A rare sign in a maritime guise, the pub at Whitby shows Captain Cook's famous vessel *Endeavour*, in which he sailed on a voyage of discovery in 1768–71. Cook learned his formidable navigational skills on the North Yorkshire coast. His title of Captain was a courtesy one as he actually achieved only the rank of Commander. Another pub with the same name at Teignmouth in Devon depicts a racing yacht called *Endeavour*.

Falmouth Packet. This sign at Germoe near Helston in Cornwall is probably unique. Falmouth was formerly a major port for regular sailings of packet-boats to the Americas and elsewhere.

Five Bells, Bourne, Lincolnshire. Bourne is well inland so it is hard to imagine that this sign refers to the nautical bells that are rung to mark the passage of time at sea. Its derivation is therefore in doubt.

Grand Junction Arms, Paddington, London W2. Close to the Paddington Basin of the Grand Junction Canal is this pub with its embossed sign. This key canal linked the industrial West Midlands to London.

Great Eastern. This sign sometimes refers to the Great Eastern Railway, which up to the early 1920s operated most of the trains in East Anglia. However, other examples commemorate the last of the ships designed by Isambard Kingdom Brunel, each of which was bigger than its predecessor and larger than any other ship afloat. The *Great Eastern* was designed to sail to Australia via the Cape of Good Hope without the need to refuel; it was fitted both with sails and with steam boilers powering paddles and screw propellers. Unsuccessful as a passenger-carrying vessel, it performed a vital role laying transatlantic communication cables.

Hope, Smithfield, London EC1. This unusual interpretation of the concept of 'hope' shows two men on a raft at sea who look as if they have spotted a possible rescue craft.

Jolly Roger. This was the flag which eighteenth-century European pirates flew when going in to make an attack. The flags were black and each pirate captain had a distinctive device designed to intimidate his victims. Popular mythology has it that they always displayed a skull and crossbones but other symbols were also used, usually suggestive of human mortality. These flags were not at all jolly and the origin of the word 'Roger' in this connection is disputed.

Jolly Sailor. There are many pubs called the 'Jolly' something. The name suggests convivial goings on in the pub. Most 'Jolly Sailors' are in coastal ports but there was a pub with this name in West Bromwich in the West Midlands, which is just about as far from the sea as you can get in Britain. It commemorated a locally-born merchant seaman who died when his ship was torpedoed in the Second World War.

Llandoger Trow. This famous pub in Bristol has a unique name. Trows were sturdy sailing barges that worked along such rivers as the Severn and Wye with commercial cargoes, which were often transferred to ocean-going vessels at Bristol. The specific barge named on this sign worked from the village of Llandogo on the Wye.

Old Blue Anchor Stores, Lowestoft, Suffolk. Both the name and the sign itself are unusual. This may be a name of dual significance. The anchor is a religious sign symbolic of security and steadfastness while blue is symbolic of hope. Additionally, the anchor was a readily recognizable symbol to mariners, of whom there were many in a town like Lowestoft, looking to the sea.

Plimsoll Arms, London N4. This unique sign recalls the 'Sailor's Friend', Samuel Plimsoll MP (1824–98), who with considerable difficulty steered the controversial Merchant Shipping Act of 1876 through Parliament. Shipping companies would scandalously send to sea overloaded 'coffin ships', which they hoped would sink, no matter whether mariners lost their lives, so that the insurance money could be claimed. After the Act was passed, the 'Plimsoll Line' had to be painted on the hulls of merchant ships indicating how much cargo could safely and legally be loaded.

Royal Sovereign. Over the centuries, a number of fighting ships of the Royal Navy have carried this name.

Ship. Many pubs with this sign are close to the sea but others can be found far inland. Some of the latter may have gained their name because an ex-mariner retired from the sea and bought a pub and wished the world to know what he had done in his earlier career. Occasionally a pub with this name may originally have been called the Noah's Ark but was renamed to suit more secular times. An attractive version of this sign adorns the pub in the village of Dunwich on the Suffolk coast. Dunwich was once an important town with many churches, but most of it has now been washed away by the sea.

Turbinia. This is a very rare sign, only two being known, both of them in the north-east of England. The pioneering vessel *Turbinia* was launched at Wallsend-on-Tyne in 1894 and was powered by a steam turbine, which not only allowed for useful fuel economies but made the vessel exceptionally fast and manoeuvrable. It raised a few eyebrows among the Royal Navy top brass but received official approval when the unconventional First Sea Lord, 'Jackie' Fisher, ordered steam turbines for HMS *Dreadnought*, the first battleship armed entirely with big guns, which revolutionised naval actions and rendered all existing battleships obsolete.

Sporting Signs

PEOPLE have always enjoyed sport, played competitively or just for fun, individually or as part of a team. Before the nineteenth century many so-called sports, using the word in the widest sense, involved cruelty to animals, and many of the others had only the most rudimentary of rules, if any, and frequently featured physical violence up to and including free-for-alls among both participants and spectators. However, in the nineteenth century, mainly because of the fear that large numbers of spectators at sporting events might get out of control, most of the activities involving cruelty to animals were abolished. Likewise, sporting events were brought under the control of national bodies administering strict rules and regulations and, with the emergence of professional players, they moved towards commercialism, becoming part of the leisure industry.

Badger Hounds, Hinderwell, North Yorkshire. This unique sign can be found in a village north of Whitby.

Baseball Tavern, Derby. This pub was adjacent to the old Derby County football stadium, which was known as The Baseball Ground as this game was also played there. In the late nineteenth century an attempt was made to introduce baseball into Britain as a summer sport but it never caught on.

Bendigo, Sneinton, Nottingham. William Abednego Thompson (1811–80), a local man, was a national champion prizefighter or 'pugilist', nicknamed 'Bendigo', a corruption of Abednego. He had two brothers called Shadrach and Meshach, all three named after biblical characters from the book of Daniel. After he retired from the ring, Bendigo became a preacher.

Bird in Hand. This familiar sign may sometimes be derived from a heraldic charge but more frequently recalls the ancient sport of falconry. An old proverb asserts that 'a bird in the hand is worth two in the bush', so there may be a droll implication that the beer is better in this pub than another pub close by, perhaps called the 'Bush'.

Dog and Duck. This sign records a distasteful sport in which a duck with pinioned wings, and therefore unable to fly, was set upon by dogs. The contest was timed, each dog having a set time in which to catch the luckless duck. The owner of a dog which was timed out bought drinks all round.

Fighting Cocks. Another leisure activity that has fortunately been banned is cock-fighting. Vast amounts of money were lost and won in wagers on the outcome of bouts between gamecocks specially bred and trained to fight. These contests sometimes took place on pub premises, hence the alternative name 'Cockpit'.

Fox and Hounds. The impact of foxhunting over centuries of British history is reflected in the great frequency of this sign throughout the country.

Gunners, London N5. Near both the former and new stadiums of Arsenal Football Club (nicknamed the Gunners), this pub displays a sign showing the club badge against a black background.

Hark to Mopsey, Normanton, West Yorkshire. A handful of pubs have a 'Hark to...' name, which commemorates famous foxhounds, leaders of the pack. Most of them are in hunting country in the north of England.

Hurdler, Stamford, Lincolnshire. This unique sign commemorates the achievements of David Cecil, Lord Burghley. He won a gold medal in the 400 metres hurdles at the 1928 Olympic Games. The impressive family seat, Burghley House, is nearby.

Larwood and Voce, West Bridgford, Nottingham. Harold Larwood played cricket for Nottinghamshire and England as a fearsome right-arm fast bowler. On the orders of his captain, Douglas Jardine, in the highly controversial series played in Australia in 1932–3, he peppered the Australian batsmen with dangerous 'bodyline' deliveries, partnered by Bill Voce, a fine fast left-arm bowler who also played for Nottinghamshire. They are remembered on this sign close to Trent Bridge cricket ground.

Maiden Over. This is a very unusual sign. The one to be seen at Earley near Reading might be construed as politically incorrect because it shows a young girl jumping over a set of cricket stumps. It is a punning sign, because a 'maiden' in the game of cricket is an over in which no runs are scored.

Sky Blue, Coventry. From 1905 to 2005 Coventry City Football Club played their home matches at the Highfield Road stadium, the pub being located close by. The name refers to the club's playing strip.

William Webb Ellis, Rugby. The boy of this name was just sixteen when he was propelled to fame. He was playing football one day on the playing fields of Rugby's famous public school when he suddenly decided to pick up the ball and carry it up the field, thereby inventing the sport of rugby. Though doubtless he was booed at the time by everyone there as a cad or even a rotter, Ellis had started something and 'rugby' soon caught on. Another pub with this name can, very appropriately, be found at Twickenham.

Yorker. An example of this rare sign, in Nottingham, showed an imposing image of the cricketer W. G. Grace on one side of the board and a lean, ascetic-looking figure on the other. This was F. R. Spofforth, known as 'the Demon'. He was the Australian fast bowler said to have invented the 'yorker', a ball bowled so as to pitch just under the bat, making it extremely difficult for the batsman to play.

Artistic Signs

THE BRITISH generally do not seem to accord their painters, sculptors, actors and writers the same respect that they receive in many other countries. They seem to have an aversion to intellectuals, and someone who gains eminence in the worlds of pop music, cinema or sport is likely to be held in much higher popular regard than a thinker or communicator of profound thoughts in such arts as poetry, painting or sculpture.

Allan Ramsay. A couple of signs in Scotland commemorate the achievements of this Scottish poet, who lived from the 1680s to 1758, although the issue is complicated because his son with the same name was a noted portrait painter.

Andrew Marvell. This pub in Hull is named after the poet (1621–78), who was born nearby. He wrote many poems with pastoral and rural themes but was also a politician, who aligned himself with the winning Parliamentary cause in the English Civil War. He became an MP and was known for his integrity, a quality not normally associated with politicians.

Augustus John, Liverpool. Born in Wales in 1878, John became a very fashionable portrait painter after for years affecting the bohemian lifestyle expected of young artists at that time. For a while he taught at Liverpool. He was elected to the Royal Academy in 1929 and died in 1961.

Ben Jonson. A few signs commemorate Jonson (1572–1637), a leading poet and dramatist. It took a long time for his work to win the praise he had hoped for, but he enjoyed a surge of popularity with various plays between 1606 and 1614. He fell out of favour with the death of James I and almost certainly died feeling that his full talent had not been appreciated.

Cartoonist, London EC1. This pub, close to Fleet Street, is unique in that it holds a competition every year for a new pictorial sign featuring a cartoon. The winner acts as the pub's sign for a year, after which it is replaced and added to the gallery of previous signs that can be seen here.

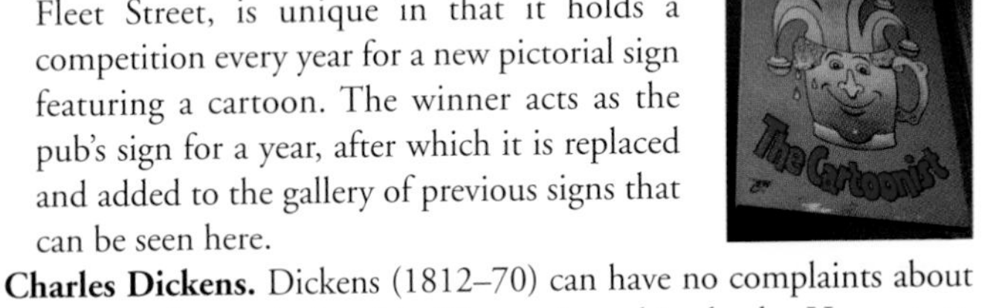

Charles Dickens. Dickens (1812–70) can have no complaints about his popularity during his life or since his death. He was an extraordinarily prolific writer who penned a succession of immensely successful novels, inventing many characters who are among the best-loved of literary creations. Stage plays, musicals, films and television dramatisations continue to keep his name in the public eye.

Gainsborough. A rare sign, this recalls the work of Thomas Gainsborough (1727–88), the English landscape and portrait painter born at Sudbury in Suffolk. Drawing inspiration from the work of Rubens and Van Dyck, he produced such well-loved paintings as *The Blue Boy* and *Mrs Siddons.* He was a founding member of the Royal Academy in 1768 but became disenchanted with the Academy when it did not always give his works the place of prominence he thought they deserved.

Gilbert and Sullivan, London WC2. William Schwenk Gilbert (1836–1911) and Arthur Seymour Sullivan (1842–1900) collaborated on a series of exceptionally successful light, mostly comic operas, for which the former wrote the libretto and the latter composed the music. Their partnership began in 1871 and concluded, triumphantly, in 1889 with *The Gondoliers.*

Laurel and Hardy, London E12. The Lancashire-born Stanley Laurel (1890–1965) and the American Oliver Hardy (1892–1957) formed a comical combination of thin man and fat man which successfully made the transition from silent films to the talkies. Their work continues to give pleasure and they unquestionably influenced many subsequent comical duos.

Lord Byron. There are several signs bearing Byron's name. George Gordon, sixth Baron Byron (1788–1824), was a larger than life character who was born lame and mistreated as a child, but as a youth and young man threw himself into a frenzy of activities, many of them dissipated, as if he was trying to make up lost time. He was a philanderer, poet, athlete and political radical with an enormous thirst for life. He supported the Greek uprising against the Turks and died of the ague at Missolonghi.

Macaulay Arms, London W8. The name refers to Thomas Babington Macaulay (1800–59), a historian and man of letters, acclaimed during his lifetime, who became a leading MP. He never allowed the facts to get in the way of a good story and his work is now criticised for containing many historical inaccuracies. In an unguarded moment in 1831, he said of a political enemy: 'I detest him more than cold boiled veal.' His political views are neatly summarised by the comment that universal suffrage would be 'utterly incompatible with the existence of civilisation'.

Old Crome, Norwich. It is fitting that John Crome (1768–1821), universally known as 'Old Crome', should be honoured with a sign in the fine city of Norwich. He was a self-taught landscape painter who helped to set up what is generally known as the Norwich School of artists, who are remembered particularly for paintings of the Norfolk countryside and the Broads, showing a strong Dutch influence. His son, also a painter, was known as 'Young Crome'.

Sir Alfred Hitchcock, London E11. Hitchcock, who was born locally in 1899 and died in 1980, was an outstanding film-maker who made a number of films in Britain in the 1930s but whose greatest work was done after he moved to Hollywood in 1939. These films include *Dial M for Murder* (1954), *Psycho* (1960) and *The Birds* (1963). Acknowledged as a master of suspense and of innovative camerawork, he made a brief and silent appearance in each of the films he directed.

Sir Walter Scott. An uncommon sign. Born in 1771 in Edinburgh and dying in 1832, Scott was an immensely prolific writer, mostly of historical novels. He had an extensive knowledge of the folklore of the Scottish border country and this is reflected in his early poetry.

He tried his hand at drama without any great success but it is for his fiction that he is best-known. He had to spend his last years writing at a frantic pace in order to earn the money to pay off debts he had accrued as a result of the collapse of a publishing company in which he was a partner. He took considerable liberties with historical detail.

Surtees. Two pubs in County Durham are named after Robert Smith Surtees (1803–64), who was born and lived much of his life locally. His best-known work was *Jorrocks's Jaunts and Jollities*, in which he follows the comic sporting activities of Mr Jorrocks, a likeable and lively cockney. This was published in 1838. Later, less well-known novels deal in considerable detail with the ups and downs of the foxhunting fraternity.

William Cobbett. Cobbett (1762–1835) was born at Farnham in Surrey, where the pub is located. Despite having to teach himself to read and write, Cobbett became a polymath. He is difficult to categorise, being an anti-democrat yet also a radical who attacked corruption and privilege wherever he found it. He wrote, edited and did just about everything else in his influential *Cobbett's Political Register*, which commenced publication in 1802. The political establishment regarded him as a gadfly and he was imprisoned for an attack on flogging in the army. *Rural Rides*, published in 1830, evokes a rural world disappearing under the twin pressures of industrialisation and urbanisation.

Railway Signs

IT IS NO EXAGGERATION to say that railways changed the world. Along with the associated electric telegraph, they began a revolution in the speed with which people, raw materials, goods and other property, as well as ideas, could be transmitted. These developments all had profound effects on the economic, social, political and cultural fabric of Britain, and the diversity of signs associated with railways is evidence of this.

Atmospheric Railway, Starcross, Devon. A number of pub names recall Isambard Kingdom Brunel (1806–59). He was a leading civil, mechanical and marine engineer with some outstanding achievements to his name, as well as a few major flops. The atmospheric railway was one of the latter. The idea was to apply this largely untried but revolutionary form of transport on the line of the South Devon Railway from Exeter to Plymouth. A number of technical problems plagued the project from the start. Expensive to build, it proved equally expensive to dismantle and replace with a conventional railway.

Brunel Arms, Crewe, Cheshire. The railway company with which Brunel is most associated is the Great Western. While it would be entirely understandable to find a pub with the name 'Brunel' in it at Swindon, the site of the company's workshops, it is very strange to find a pub with this name at Crewe, which was the base of one of its rivals, the London & North Western Railway. Of the three railway companies that ran trains into Crewe, the LNWR ran the vast majority; the other two companies, the North Staffordshire and the Great Western, had a very minor presence. Was this pub named by someone cocking a snook at the LNWR?

Crab and Winkle, Werrington, Peterborough. This unique sign may be an example of a little knowledge being a dangerous thing. A railway line operated by the Midland & Great Northern Railway ran from Peterborough carrying holiday-makers to the seaside delights of Cromer, Sheringham and Great Yarmouth. This line was nicknamed 'The Crab and Winkle'. However it ran a couple of miles nearer the city centre of Peterborough. Much closer to the pub was a line built by the Great Northern Railway which took pleasure-seekers to Lincolnshire resorts such as Skegness but it was never called the 'Crab and Winkle'.

EUR, Ipswich. One of the shortest pub names, this would be a puzzle unless the observer knew that it stood for the Eastern Union Railway, which had a station nearby. The EUR was later absorbed into the Eastern Counties Railway, which was not only impecunious but by all accounts thoroughly incompetent as well. This in turn became part of the Great Eastern Railway, which made a better job of serving East Anglia. The pub was known locally as 'Ere You Are'.

Evening Star. One or two houses with this name display a sign showing no. 92220 'Evening Star' which was the last steam locomotive to be built for what was then British Railways. It left Swindon Works brand new in March 1960. Her appropriate, even poignant, name was chosen as the result of a competition.

George Stephenson, Killingworth, Tyne and Wear. Stephenson (1781–1848), who was born close by, is regarded as the 'Father of the Railways' for his achievements in the construction of railways and the design and building of steam locomotives, the most notable of which was *Rocket*, which ran away with the prize at the Rainhill Trials, held near Liverpool in 1829. This was a competition to decide what kind of locomotive should operate on the Liverpool & Manchester Railway, soon to be opened.

Gluepot. This is an unusual sign which, in the case of the example at Swindon, refers to the work of the upholsterers who laboured in the town's railway carriage and wagon workshops. The Gluepot at Swindon is located in a 'village' built by the Great Western Railway to house its workers and it is likely that many of the upholsterers would have lived close by and used this establishment.

Great Western. The size of the Great Western's network means that there are many signs around this theme. A good example showing the artist's knowledge of interesting everyday detail could be found at West Bromwich, West Midlands. It depicted a 2-6-2 tank engine of the 45xx class being watered, with the driver on the platform controlling the supply and the fireman placing the leather 'bag' in the top of the locomotive's side tank.

Light Railway, Hulme End, Staffordshire. The light railway referred to was an eccentric narrow-gauge line called the Leek & Manifold Valley, which ran through delightful countryside in the western part of the Peak District. It opened in 1904 and was built with the intention of tapping the potential for tourist traffic. Hulme End was the eastern terminus. The line ran out of steam in 1934.

Locomotive. This is a fairly common sign. Sometimes the painter gives full rein to his artistic talent but at the expense of historical accuracy. He may paint a virtuoso depiction of a locomotive – but one which never ran anywhere near the pub concerned. For example, he might show a Great Western 'King' Class locomotive on a sign in East Anglia. Occasionally the sign may show another kind of steam locomotive such as a road traction engine.

Midland Railway. The Midland Railway Company, whose headquarters were at Derby, was arguably the biggest of the railway companies before the amalgamation or 'Grouping' into the 'Big Four', which the government imposed on the railways in 1923. The company extended its tentacles into places as far apart as Carlisle, Swansea, Bath, London, Peterborough, Lincoln, Manchester, Birmingham, Morecambe and Leeds. The size of the system accounts for the large number of names relating to this company.

Pride of Paddington, Praed Street, London W2. Paddington was the London terminus of the Great Western Railway, which probably had more devotees than any other British railway company.

Railway, Aldeburgh, Suffolk. Aldeburgh was the terminus of a rather inconsequential branch line from Saxmundham. The line closed decades ago. The sign shows a train on the narrow gauge Southwold Railway that was a feature of Suffolk until it closed in 1929.

Railway Swan, Bedford. This sign shows a very curious juxtaposition of themes. Pubs with names of this sort are usually the result of the amalgamation of two houses and the incorporation of elements of both names in the survivor. This pub is, or was, near Bedford St John's station.

Silent Whistle. This rather poignant name can occasionally be found adorning a pub near a closed railway station or defunct railway line. Sometimes it represents a change from an earlier name such as 'Railway Tavern' or 'Station Inn'. Contrary to popular perception, closures of lines or individual stations had been going on long before Dr Beeching took charge in the 1960s.

Silver Jubilee. This unusual sign sometimes refers to royal anniversaries. The pub with this name at Peterborough, however, is near the East Coast Main Line, along which in the 1930s ran this glamorous express, hauled by a streamlined Gresley 'Pacific' locomotive.

Spyglass & Kettle, near Gillingham, Kent. This curious and whimsical name is the result of the merging of two pubs, one being the 'Lord Nelson' and the other the 'Steam Engine'.

Fighting Heroes

ALL PARTS of the British Isles have been vulnerable to invasion and the kingdom as a whole has often felt threatened by possible attacks from the sea. Especially from the eighteenth century onwards, Britain has been involved in the development of colonies and international trading links. Rivalries with other nations doing the same led to almost continuous warfare in one part of the world or another. All this has given ample scope for fighting men and women to be commemorated in pub signs and names. Those immortalised in this way have mostly been senior officers.

Admiral Blake. Robert Blake (1599–1657) was a country squire from Somerset who became an MP in the 1630s and fought with distinction on the Parliamentary side in the Civil War on land. In 1649 he was appointed Admiral and went on to a glorious career on the seas against the Royalists and against the Dutch and Spanish. London W8 has a pub bearing his name but, as with similar heroes, other pubs make varied reference to him.

Captain Mannering, Shoeburyness, Essex. It is not known whether this is a deliberate misspelling but the 'hero' referred to here was the much-loved Captain Mainwaring of the long-running television comedy series *Dad's Army*. Incompetent, pompous and totally lacking in humour, Mainwaring nevertheless had the kind of back-to-the-wall determination and dignity that underpinned the efforts of the Home Guard in the Second World War. He was played brilliantly by Arthur Lowe.This pub has now been renamed The Garrison Arms.

Churchill Arms, Kensington, London W8. Sir Winston Churchill was and remains a controversial character. His heroic status derives from his leadership of Britain to victory in the Second World War.

Duke of Wellington. This common sign commemorates Arthur Wellesley (1769–1852), created Duke of Wellington in recognition of his outstanding success in a long military career, culminating in the final but close-run defeat of Napoleon Bonaparte at Waterloo in 1815. Wellesley then entered politics as a Tory, becoming increasingly irascible and reactionary as he got older. In particular, his opposition to any extension of the franchise made him extremely unpopular and led to the stoning of his London house. He was nicknamed the 'Iron Duke' because of his inflexible discipline. There are several Iron Duke pubs.

Earl of Cardigan, Norwich. James Thomas Brudenell (1797–1868) bought a commission in the Army in 1830 and soon found himself in command of the 15th Hussars – just like that. His fiery temper made him unpopular wherever he went but did not prevent him being promoted to Major-General. In the Crimean War he led the charge of the Light Brigade at the Battle of Balaklava in 1854, which was immortalised in a poem by Lord Tennyson as an example of gung-ho bravery combined with monumental stupidity and contempt on the part of the senior command for the lives of the soldiers for whom they were responsible.

Earl St Vincent. A handful of signs recall John Jervis (1735–1823). He was fourteen when he joined his first ship and he went on to enjoy an exceptionally fine career, the high spot of which was probably his victory off Cape St Vincent in 1797 over a combined French, Dutch and Spanish fleet. He was a strict, even harsh disciplinarian and had no truck with the men who mutinied in 1797 and 1798. He was a crabby old martinet, both feared and respected by those who had contact with him, but it was to his credit that he recognised the potential of Horatio Nelson and used his patronage to assist the latter's career.

General Havelock. A few pub names recall Sir Henry Havelock (1795–1857), whose military actions were mostly in the Middle East and in India. During the Indian Mutiny in 1857 and 1858 he won several engagements against the rebel troops and led the relief of the garrison at Lucknow. Like many of his men, he was struck down by dysentery. Brave he may have been, but historians generally now have less respect for Britain's role in the history of the Indian sub-continent and he is no longer a 'fashionable' hero.

Hero of Aliwal, Whittlesey, Cambs. The eponymous 'hero' was Sir Harry Smith, born locally. Smith led a force which inflicted a heavy defeat on the rebel Sikh forces near Lahore in 1846.

John Paul Jones. Regarded by some as a renegade, Jones, who was born in Scotland, made a name for himself as a commander in the American navy at the time of the revolution in the 1770s. He led a raid on Whitehaven, Cumbria, in 1778.

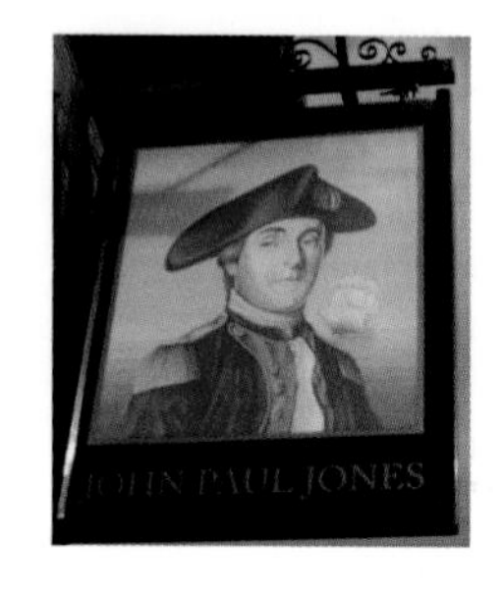

Leefe Robinson, Harrow Weald, Middlesex. This young member of the Royal Flying Corps fought a battle in the skies with a German Zeppelin airship in September 1916 and eventually shot it down in flames near Cuffley in Hertfordshire. He won the Victoria Cross for what was described as an attack carried out in difficult and dangerous circumstances. Some might say that anyone who took off in the flimsy fighting planes of the time deserved a medal but his action in being the first to bring down a Zeppelin showed that these sinister and silent killers were not invulnerable.

Marquis of Granby. This is a common sign found scattered throughout Britain and it honours the memory of John Manners (1721–70), the Marquis of Granby, who held high command in the British army in the middle of the eighteenth century. He was noted for his personal courage and his leadership from the front, which fact was recognised and applauded by those who served under him. On one occasion he was leading a charge when his wig blew off and many stories, possibly apocryphal, stem from this. Unusually concerned about the welfare of his men, he bought pubs for many of his NCOs when they retired, either through injury or ill health, and they marked their gratitude by naming the hostelries concerned after the Marquis. Tony Weller, a favourite Dickens character from *The Pickwick Papers*, owned a pub called the Marquis of Granby.

Sir Alexander Fleming, Paddington, London W2. Fleming (1881–1955) fought to save lives and discovered penicillin. It is good to see such an outstanding development remembered by a pub sign.

Sir Garnet Wolseley, Norwich. Born in 1833, Wolseley rose to the rank of Field Marshal, having made a name for himself in innumerable campaigns, including that in the Sudan in the 1880s.

Sir James Borlase Warren, Nottingham. This sign celebrates the very distinguished career of the locally-born Warren, who was a distinguished naval officer in the wars against the French in the late eighteenth and early nineteenth centuries. He rose to the rank of admiral but never caught the public imagination in the same way as some of the other 'sea-dogs' of the great days of fighting sail.

Van Tromp, London, E2. It is rare for a foreign hero, let alone an enemy, to give his name to a British pub. Maarten Harpertszoon Tromp (1597–1653) was a Dutch admiral who commanded the fleet during the first Anglo-Dutch War. His arch-rival was Admiral Blake, mentioned above. Honours were roughly even over a number of encounters between Tromp and the English navy, despite the fact that the English forces were more powerful and better equipped. It was probably fitting that he died in battle against his old enemy.

Mammal Signs

MANKIND has a confused and highly complex relationship with the animal kingdom. We kill animals for food, and sometimes for pleasure; we utilise their skills and strengths for a wide variety of purposes; we bully and even torture them; but we can be killed or harmed by animals from the very largest through to microscopic pathogens. We write about them in literature and represent them in painting and sculpture; we even make gods of them. We can develop close personal and mutually affectionate relationships with animals. We go to great lengths to conserve them and yet fight other humans in order to seize their fur or other valuable products. We endow them with human qualities – for example, foxes are thought of as cunning, lions as noble and fierce, donkeys as stupid. It is hardly surprising that animals feature in a large and wide range of pub signs and names.

Bear. Many pub names with 'bear' in them are likely to have been derived from the arms of a great landowning family. The various colours describing the bears on signs are usually references to these heraldic charges. Heraldry has its own technical language or jargon, such as 'gules' meaning red, 'azure' for blue and 'sable' for black. However, these have never caught on in wider society and there are, for example, no pubs named the Sable Bear. Nearly all bears on signs are muzzled, indicative of their role as baited bears.

Bleeding Wolf. Two pubs in Cheshire have this unusual name, possibly associated with the killing of the last wild wolf in England. That at Hale had a bus stop outside it and the author remembers that some fastidious passengers could not bear to ask for the stop by its correct name, because they did not want to use an expletive. A bleeding wolf was a motif displayed on the arms of the Earls of Chester.

Buck. This refers to the fallow deer. It is not a particularly common theme for signs but there are at least one Bald Buck, White Buck and Running Buck. Unique is Buck in the Park at Derby, which is taken from the coat of arms of the city. Ormskirk in Lancashire had a Buck in the Vine.

Bull. This beast comes in a variety of colours, most commonly perhaps Black, Brown, Red and White. Unique is a Blue Bull, one of many 'blue' signs around Grantham in Lincolnshire, where much land was once owned by the Manners family. Bull's Head is often derived from the arms of Henry VIII, known as a serial ignorer of indignant papal bulls. The Flying Bull at Rake in Hampshire is the name of a stagecoach. Bull and Stirrup is a unique sign at Chester. Another unique sign in Essex is Bullocks. Stamford in Lincolnshire has a Bull and Swan, while there are several houses called Bull and Butcher.

Cat. This creature, which generally looks down on humankind, appears on signs in a number of guises. One of the most familiar is Cat and Fiddle. The origin of this name is obscure. Cheshire Cat at Ellesmere Port, Cheshire, is probably unique. Lewis Carroll in *Alice's Adventures in Wonderland* picks up the old idea of grinning Cheshire cats and Alice encounters a large, friendly and grinning, if somewhat contrary, cat sitting in a tree. There are at least two pubs named 'Fat Cat', one of which shows a flashy-looking cat with a big cigar and an expensive suit. The sign of the Squinting Cat at Pannal, North Yorkshire, incorporates reflectors as the eyes of the cat.

Dog. Another ever-present domestic animal, the dog occasionally appears just as 'the Dog' but more often in combinations, such as Dog and Duck, Dog and Gun, or Dog and Partridge. Occasionally a specific breed is shown on a sign, such as Border Terrier or Bulldog. Some 'dog' signs probably have a religious origin since in biblical terms the dog is symbolic of watchfulness and fidelity. There are a small number of coloured dogs including Red, White and Golden ones. The former Dog and Bear at Nottingham was a reminder of bear-baiting. At Keswick, Cumbria, can be found Twa Dogs, an obscure reference to a poem by Robert Burns.

Dun Cow. In pre-industrial Britain, many livelihoods depended on farmyard beasts. This sign celebrates the fact.

Elephant. For an exotic animal that is not indigenous to Britain, elephants feature in pub names with surprising frequency. Perhaps most familiar is the Elephant and Castle sign, the origin of which is disputed. A favourite explanation is that the depiction of an elephant with a howdah on its back is a reference to these animals being used as war machines in the Crusades. Some say the name refers to a beautiful medieval Spanish princess, the Infanta de Castile, and has been corrupted so that the English could pronounce it. The device appears on the arms of the Cutlers' Company, who used ivory for the handles of the knives and forks they made.

Fox, Hoxton, London N1. This London street-corner pub has a fine tiled sign.

Horse. There are many names with equine associations. Horses on pub signs come in a variety of colours such as Bay, Black, Golden, Grey and Sorrel. They are also common in combination, for example Horse and Panniers, Horse and Farrier, and Horse and Trumpet. There is an Old Roan in north Liverpool, which gives its name to the surrounding district, and innumerable Nag's Heads, some of which defy political correctness by showing a quarrelsome woman. Rampant Horse, Suffolk, is presumably an heraldic item. In heraldry the horse symbolises speed and bravery.

Lion. The lion is symbolic of strength, majesty and courage. Legend has it that lion cubs are born dead and only come to life three days after birth when their sire breathes on them. Some 'lion' signs are therefore of religious origin because the lion symbolises the Resurrection. Most signs, however, are probably heraldic in origin and therefore lions come in a wide range of colours, including Black, Blue, Brown, Golden, Red, White and Yellow. Five Lions at York refers to the arms of the city. Two Lions, at Penrith, Cumbria, is an unusual variation .

Ox. Uncommonly shown on signs, the ox is the symbol of strength and patience in biblical terms. A Fat Ox features on several signs in the north-east of England. Seemingly, the animal comes in only Black or Grey and the most common theme for the sign is probably a breed or a specific prizewinning animal. Examples are Ketton Ox, Yarm, North Yorkshire, and Swiss Ox, Berwick, Sussex.

Squinting Cat, Pannal Ash, Harrogate. The name is not unique but the sign of this particular house certainly is. It shows a rather tortured-looking cat with reflectors for eyes.

Birds, Fish and Other Creatures

THERE are many signs featuring birds. Man has found myriad uses for birds which are reflected in pub names, but they also feature on large numbers of signs of heraldic or religious origin. Fewer signs show fish but there are enough of them to provide evidence of the complex relationships that man has with these creatures. This section starts, however, with an oddity related to insects.

Beehive. Although the name is not unique, the sign of the Beehive, close to the town centre of Grantham, Lincolnshire, is unique – it is the only living pub sign. At the front of the pub is a sizeable tree with a hive containing live bees. There is an inscription which reads:

Stop, traveller, this wondrous sign explore
And say when thou hast viewed it o'er
Grantham, now, two rarities are thine –
A lofty steeple and a living sign.

Cock. This comes in many guises and is often an indication that cock-fighting took place on the premises. Fighting Cocks is an obvious example, as is Cockpit. Sometimes the name includes the location, such as Cock o' Tupsley in Herefordshire. Some signs may be of religious origin. The cock, because it crows early in the morning, is emblematic of watchfulness. It is also one of the symbols of Christ's Passion.

Crane. This bird features only rarely on signs and sometimes the board shows the bird on one side and the lifting apparatus on the other. In biblical terms the crane symbolises vigilance, loyalty and an upright life. In legend, the crane is always watchful because it stands on one leg while holding a stone in the foot of its other leg. If it nods off, it relaxes and the stone falls on to its standing foot, thereby waking it up.

Dolphin. The dolphin is a mammal but it is included here because it was thought of as a fish for heraldic purposes. Because of its intelligence and apparent affinity with humans, it is held in high regard and appears on many signs. Mariners believed that it saved ships during stormy weather by wrapping itself around the anchor and stopping it from dragging. Dolphins feature on the coats of arms of two livery companies, the Fishmongers and the Watermen and Lightermen. Occasionally it appears in combination, such as the erstwhile Bull and Dolphin at Peterborough.

Dove. In ecclesiastical art, the dove is a symbol of purity and peace, hence Dove and Olive Branch at Hale, Cheshire. The Guild of Tallow Chandlers displayed three doves, each bearing an olive branch in its beak, and some signs including a dove may derive from their armorial bearings.

Goose. A goose was the symbol of St Laurence, who was roasted on a gridiron by the Romans as a martyr for his Christian beliefs. The Goose and Gridiron was an ancient pub in the City of London, the gridiron being the saint's other symbol. Its signboard can be seen in the Museum of London with many other old and interesting signs.

Goose and Cuckoo, Rhyd-y-Meirch, Monmouthshire. The distinctive sign of this pub is supposed to have originated with a nickname by which it was referred to locally and which eventually became the official name.

Iron Devil. This former pub at Sheffield had a unique name which provides a fine example of linguistic corruption. The wealthy Howard family owned much land in this part of Yorkshire. Their coat of arms featured a swallow – *hirondelle* in French. Such a word was difficult for the locals to pronounce, so it evolved into 'Iron Devil', by no means inappropriate for a city that built its economy on iron and steel.

Parrot. Though not indigenous to Britain, parrots are popular as pets and in a few places they have escaped and gone feral. They appear on a small number of signs. Their colourful plumage lends itself to the signwriter's art and a fanciful but eye-catching example is the Parrot and Punchbowl at Aldringham in Suffolk.

Peregrine, Chaddesden, Derby. This newish pub was given a unique and appropriate name because peregrines have nested on the lofty tower of Derby Cathedral for several years. These formidable raptors can doubtless find plenty of urban pigeons to satisfy their hunger. Although only a couple of inches bigger than a pigeon, a peregrine's attack can be a one-sided affair since it is estimated that the latter, when swooping for the kill, can reach a speed of up to 180 mph.

Pike. This superbly designed predator of pond, river and lake is honoured in a few signs, often in a combination such as Pike and Heron, north of Sheffield, and two pubs called Pike and Eel in Cambridgeshire. The city of Cambridge has a Pickerel, which is a young pike. In the northern counties a pub name with a 'pike' element in it may provide a view of a prominent hill. Pike and Musket refers to the military weapon.

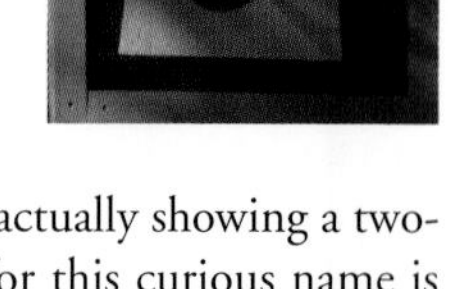

Sea Horse. This curious but charming little fish is celebrated on a handful of signs. Occasionally the sign depicts a mythical creature whose front quarters resembled a horse while the hind quarters were those of a fish.

Swan. Swans are admired for their beauty on water, although definitely not on land. Swans appear on a number of heraldic achievements including those of Edward III and Henry VIII. A few pubs sport the sign 'Swan with Two Necks', even on occasions actually showing a two-necked swan. One beguiling explanation for this curious name is that it refers to the swans which were marked with two nicks in their beaks to indicate that they belonged to the Worshipful Company of Vintners. Various sign-painters, unaware of this practice of 'nicking', thought they would put 'Swan with Two Nicks' right when repainting a sign. 'Black Swan' pubs are usually nicknamed 'Mucky Duck' or 'Dirty Duck'.

Folklore and Legend

STORYTELLING and the oral tradition were, and to some extent remain, important means whereby culture has been transmitted from one generation to another and across nations around the world. Many of the stories enjoyed by successive generations over centuries have absolutely no grounding in reality but this has not diminished their popularity, especially in a world increasingly dominated by the apparent certainties and rationalities of science and technology.

Apollo. There are a few pubs with this name. In Greek mythology, Apollo was the god of music, poetry, archery, prophecy and the healing arts. He was also the epitome of perfect young manhood. Because of his role in healing, he features on the arms of the Worshipful Company of Apothecaries. When the world was excited by news of the Apollo space probes, there was a surge in the number of pubs with this name.

Bladud's Head. This unique sign is at Larkhall in Bath. The story goes that Bladud, son of Hudibras, king of the ancient Britons, contracted leprosy and was forced to leave home. He became a swineherd but passed on the leprosy to his pigs. One day he saw them plunge into some boggy marshland; when they came out they were cured of their affliction. Eagerly Bladud then plunged into the mud and he too was cured. In gratitude he later founded a settlement where this had happened and this was the origin of Bath.

Cuckoo Bush. A well-known legend in Nottinghamshire relates how in the early thirteenth century King John sent his surveyors to the

Gotham area to find land to be reserved as a royal hunting forest. The villagers were opposed to the idea and so they decided to feign madness, to put the surveyors off. They performed a number of stunts such as admiring a cuckoo sitting on a bush. They liked it so much that they built a fence around the bush to stop the cuckoo flying away; as soon as the fence was complete, the bird took to the wing. This and similar stupidities did the trick and King John kept well away.

Golden Fleece. The name is a reference to the Greek legend in which the Argonauts sought the Golden Fleece.

Green Man. This is a common sign but its origins are wrapped in mystery. 'Green men' abound in ecclesiastical art and are thought to be pagan fertility spirits, suitably modified for Christian purposes. Carvings of green men, usually depicted with foliage emerging from their ears, nose and mouth, can frequently be found in old churches. Sometimes the sign shows a wild man of the woods or Robin Hood dressed in his Lincoln green.

John Barleycorn. This rare sign is a personification of the spirit of any beer based on barley. In a number of curious folk-tales John Barleycorn becomes a kind of champion of the ordinary people and of all things English.

King Arthur. Several pubs feature the name of this figure, who is surrounded by so many legends. One of these pubs is at Glastonbury in Somerset. There are many associations with Arthur in the locality; they are a mixture of history and folklore, pagan myth and Christian fantasy. Many of our perceptions of him are based on *Morte d'Arthur*, written by Sir Thomas Mallory and published in 1485. In the twelfth century the monks of Glastonbury Abbey claimed that they had found Arthur's bones.

King Lud. This well-known pub in London EC4, near the old Ludgate, is now closed. Lud is supposed to have been a king of the ancient Britons who heroically rallied his people for the fight against foreign invaders. It is claimed that he founded London around 66 BC.

Robin Hood. This is a very common sign found throughout Britain. The outlaw Robin is a traditional folk hero of English ballads. The first mention of him seems to be in Langland's *The Vision of Piers Plowman,* which appeared in 1377. Folklorists and historians cannot agree whether he actually existed or, if he did, who he was and when he lived. However, a very engaging concept has developed of the outlaw, perhaps of noble birth but wrongfully deprived of his birthright, who took to the forests with a band of likeable rakehells and proceeded to rob hated oppressors of the ordinary people, preferably corrupt sheriffs and bloated bishops. He then took most of what he had extracted from these oppressors and disbursed it among the poor and needy.

Straw Bear. This unique name at Whittlesey, Cambridgeshire, celebrates the town's Straw Bear Festival, held annually in January. It takes place over three days starting on the Tuesday after Plough Monday. Traditionally, a ploughman is dressed up to look something like a bear covered in straw. To the accompaniment of music, he is led through the streets dancing and begging for food, drink and money. Killjoy magistrates closed the festival down in 1909 but it was revived in 1980 and is still going strong.

Turpin's Cave. Close to Epping Forest, where Dick Turpin is supposed to have had a hideaway, this pub is at Loughton in Essex. A myth has developed around highwaymen, and Turpin in particular, that they were handsome and courteous and robbed almost reluctantly but made amends by giving some of what they stole to needy widows and other indigent members of the underclass. Nothing could be further from the truth. Turpin was an ugly, violent and brutal desperado who never gave anything away. Nor did he make a heroic headlong dash on his horse Black Bess from London to York to establish an alibi. An earlier highwayman did indeed perform such a deed but it was the novelist Harrison Ainsworth (1805–82) who attributed the feat to Turpin in *Rookwood*, published in 1834.

Literary Signs

PERHAPS it is strange that we all like a good read even if we know what we are reading about is entirely imaginary. Some characters from fiction and literature have become extremely popular and there is no doubt that some people think that they actually existed. For example, the Sherlock Holmes Society of London receives large numbers of enquiries from people at their wit's end imploring the imaginary sleuth to apply his razor-sharp intellect and methods to solving such problems as tracing their missing cat, finding the miscreants who burgled their home and how to guarantee winning on the National Lottery.

Betsey Trotwood, London EC1. She appears in Charles Dickens's *David Copperfield* as the great-aunt of the eponymous David. She is a staunch friend to him and, although she is over eighty years of age at the end, she is tough and thinks nothing of walking miles through the countryside for pleasure or on business.

Bilbo Baggins. This unique sign at Eastbourne celebrates a small, hairy-footed creature, outwardly cowardly but with inner reserves of intelligence and fortitude. Bilbo is the hero of Tolkien's novel *The Hobbit, or There and Back Again*, which was published in 1937. Along with the wizard Gandalf and a motley collection of dwarfs, he helps to slay a dragon and recover a hoard of treasure. Bristol has a Tap and Hobbit.

Black Beauty. This pub near Scunthorpe recalls the horse which acts both as narrator and the central character in Anna Sewell's well-loved novel *Black Beauty*, published in 1877. Many generations of children have warmed to this sentimental story with a happy outcome. At the time, the Royal Society for the Prevention of Cruelty to Animals found it powerful enough to use as propaganda and it may well have assisted in improving the treatment of carriage horses in late-Victorian England.

Jekyll and Hyde. This is a rare sign. In *The Strange Case of Dr Jekyll and Mr Hyde*, the novel by Robert Louis Stevenson published in 1886, Dr Henry Jekyll is a conscientious doctor who is aware of the duality of good and evil in all humans. From time to time he brews a medicinal potion which transforms him into the villainous Mr Hyde, through whom he manifests all the evil in himself. The problem is that the evil *alter ego* gradually gains the ascendancy and commits an awful murder. Jekyll experiences the horrors of being less and less able to return to his original form and character and, aware that he is about to be discovered, he commits suicide.

Lorna Doone. A rare name, this recalls the heroine of R. D. Blackmore's historical novel *Lorna Doone, a Romance of Exmoor*, published in 1869. This melodramatic tale concerns two families, the Doones, who are brigands, and their enemies the Ridds, and the events that occur after Lorna saves the life of John Ridd. It is set in the mid-1680s.

Robinson Crusoe. The sign is rare but the story familiar. *The Life and Strange Adventures of Robinson Crusoe* by Daniel Defoe was published in 1719. It was based on the experiences of Alexander Selkirk, who ran away to sea in 1704, joined a privateer and was voluntarily put ashore on a supposedly uninhabited island, where he displayed great resourcefulness in finding ways to survive.

Sherlock Holmes. This pub in London WC2 is a shrine to the memory of a fictional character. One of the most popular and enduring literary creations, Holmes is unmistakeable in the minds of most people, probably because of the artist Sidney Paget, who provided the illustrations when many of the Holmes stories appeared in serial form in the *Strand* magazine. Tall, lean and with an aquiline

nose, Holmes possessed formidable powers of observation, analysis and deduction, which enabled him to solve almost every mystery that came his way. On the negative side, he could be intolerant of those with slower intellectual faculties, was untidy and resorted to narcotics when suffering from recurrent bouts of depression or boredom. Also, he played the violin with more enthusiasm than virtuosity.

Three Men in a Boat, Walsall, West Midlands. The name recalls the best-known novel written by the locally-born Jerome K. Jerome (1859–1927). Published in 1889, it was the immensely successful story of three likeable rapscallions and their dog who take a boating holiday on the River Thames.

Trade and Occupational Signs

PUB NAMES should never be changed lightly. Too often, the marketing people at breweries and pub-owning companies change the name of a pub and replace it with some meaningless banality that they think may attract new custom among the young drinkers who are their target market. Any increase in trade which follows is usually short-lived, and frequently the name and the style of the pub then undergo another change. The old name, however, may have been a genuine piece of historical evidence highlighting some crucial aspect of the past of that particular locality. Trade signs do not fit with modern 'images' and are frequently victims of these crass practices.

Artizan, Northampton. This sign shows a man working in the shoemaking industry, with which this town was associated.

Banker, London EC4. The role of bankers has come under considerable critical scrutiny in the twenty-first century. This sign shows a bewigged man, presumably a 'fat cat' banker, eagerly carving a large roast fowl. He will be able to slake the thirst he works up doing the carving by quaffing from the large glass of claret that is also shown. London SE1 has a Barrow Boy and Banker, which could be taken as implying a connection between the two occupations.

Bowlturners' Arms, Leicester. This is likely to refer to the local workers who used to fashion bowls for use in a sport that has been popular for centuries.

Brewer and Firkin, West Hartlepool, County Durham. This shows a brewer with part of his stock-in-trade.

Engineers' Arms. A rare sign, the example at Salisbury showed a man working away at a bench in a workshop where steam locomotives were maintained. At Heywood in Lancashire the sign shows a trade certificate issued by the Amalgamated Society of Engineers, a pioneer in the 1850s of trade unions for small groups of highly skilled and well-paid workers.

Fleece. England's early industrial wealth was largely based on the rearing of sheep and the export of raw wool and, later, finished cloth.

Framesmiths' Arms, Bulwell, Nottingham. The industrial prosperity of Nottingham in the eighteenth and nineteenth centuries was based largely on the hosiery and lace industries. These both went through a very painful transformation from small-scale domestic craft production to modern high-output mechanised methods needing little skill in the operatives. An ancillary industry developed constructing the frames or machines required by the industries.

Jet Miners, Great Broughton, North Yorkshire. Jet is the fossilised wood of an ancient tree of the same family as the present-day Araucaria, familiarly known as the monkey puzzle. These trees grew during the Jurassic period about 180 million years ago. When the trees died, they fell into swamps before being washed out to sea, where they drifted to the bottom. Other material piled on top, crushing the remnants and causing chemical changes which created jet. Jet was enormously popular as a material used for jewellery and ornaments during the Victorian period. There were many jet mines along the coast north of Whitby and inland in the North Yorkshire Moors.

Jolly Buffer, Sheffield. This unique name refers to one of the trades within the local cutlery industry, whereby the buffer polished the cutlery to a glistening shine.

Jolly Colliers, Coalville, Leicestershire. This town, as its name suggests, was built on coal, or at least the mining of it. The sign showed a group of pitmen going to work and waiting for the cage to take them down into the bowels of the earth.

Lamplighters, Shirehampton, Bristol. This pub is named after a local eighteenth-century businessman called Joseph Swetman who became rich on the profits he made from gaining the contract for looking after the oil lamps in the city of Bristol. There are a couple of Lamplighter pubs. One of them, appropriately, is in Edinburgh, for it was in the city's elegant New Town that Robert Louis Stevenson wrote his delightful short poem 'The Lamplighter'. It is about a small boy who watches the man lighting the lamps every evening and decides that when he is grown up he too will become a lamplighter.

Ship and Trades, Chatham, Kent. The sign and name recall the vital role played by the Chatham naval dockyard in refitting ships, but especially in providing the vital supplies of food and materials required to keep the vessels of the Royal Navy at sea.

Steelmelters Arms, near Chesterfield, Derbyshire. The pub recalls an ironworks in the vicinity which closed down in the twentieth century.

Three Compasses, Smithfield, London EC1. This device appears on the arms of the livery companies of Joiners, Carpenters and Masons.

Waterman's Arms. Watermen owned and operated the water taxis of yesteryear. Those who operated on the Thames in London had the reputation of being an awkward group of men. Taking advantage of the fact that travel on the river was far preferable to trying to move around London's streets, they systematically overcharged those who were not prepared to stand up to them. The sign at the pub with this name at Brixham in Devon provides an unexpected image of a man with a yoke carrying two buckets – presumably of water.

Wheeltappers. There were a tiny handful of pubs celebrating this redundant occupation. The wheeltapper used to make his way at track level down the side of an express train that was calling at a major station. He would tap the carriage wheels with a special hammer and could tell by the sound that it made whether there was any defect that would require the carriage to be removed from the train.

Whitesmiths' Arms. An unusual sign. The whitesmiths either worked with tin and other light metals, or they polished and burnished them.

Food and Drink

MOST PUBS now dispense food. Older readers may remember that back in the 1970s pub fare was sometimes restricted to crisps, salted peanuts and perhaps sandwiches or the occasional pie of dubious provenance and age. Fortunately, that situation has changed and Britain's pubs now serve food providing for every taste and budget. Many pubs reflect the role of food and drink in social history and popular culture.

Baron of Beef. An uncommon sign, this refers to a cut of beef consisting of a double sirloin joined at the backbone. It may have indicated that wholesome food was available on the premises.

Bass House. A handful of pubs had this name. The Bass brewery was established at Burton upon Trent, Staffordshire, in 1777 and its products went on to be available throughout Britain and to be extensively exported. One of the most famous was India Pale Ale (IPA), which was developed to quench the thirsts of the large number of British expatriates who administered the Indian Raj during the nineteenth and early twentieth centuries. The numerous brewers at Burton drew their water supplies from aquifers filtered through measures of gypsum. These were particularly suitable for the brewing of light, sparkling beers.

Bramley Apple, Southwell, Nottinghamshire. This unique name is found on a pub in the delightful small town which huddles around Southwell Minster, one of England's least-known cathedrals. The apple is more correctly known as 'Bramley's Seedling'.

Café Royal, Edinburgh. With a name that suggests it is a different kind of catering establishment, this is architecturally one of the most magnificent of Britain's pubs. With luxurious Victorian fittings and tiled mural pictures, it was at one time a showroom for sanitary ware. Perhaps the Café Royal in London provided the inspiration for the name because it was a meeting place for writers and painters.

Cheshire Cheese. This aristocrat among English cheeses gives its name to a number of pubs, including the famous and historic Ye Olde Cheshire Cheese in London's Fleet Street. It is thought that Cheshire cheese was being made before the Romans arrived in Britain and it is mentioned in the Domesday survey of the late eleventh century. The cheese was exported overseas in the Middle Ages but the development of canals and later of railways made it available virtually throughout Britain.

Frying Pan. There are only a couple of examples of this name. It is likely that these pubs were located in premises previously used by ironmongers, who might well have drawn attention to the retail services they provided by using an extra large frying pan as a shop sign.

Greengage, Bury St Edmunds, Suffolk. This now uncommon variety of plum was publicised in the early nineteenth century by Sir William Gage. The greengage caught on but his attempts to promote a 'bluegage' and a 'purplegage' were unsuccessful.

Orange Tree. A few pubs display this name. Oranges are a citrus fruit native to China and south-east Asia and were probably introduced into Britain in the late sixteenth century. Many other exotic flowers, fruit and plants appeared in Britain in the following centuries and made a considerable impression. Special glass buildings were erected so that oranges could be cultivated here in small numbers by the rich.

Oxnoble. Two pubs, both in Greater Manchester, sport this name, which refers to a type of potato, once popular but since largely replaced by more productive strains.

Pigeon Pie, Sherburn-in-Elmet, North Yorkshire. This delicacy, not perhaps to everyone's taste these days, was an example of the way in which our thrifty ancestors were able to make the most of nature's largesse. Other birds, now disdained as food, that formed the main constituents in pies included moorhen, rook and, of course, blackbird.

Plum Tree. This pub at Pershore in Worcestershire is in an area renowned for its orchards. Winchester has a Pershore Plum pub.

Queen's Head and Artichoke, London NW1. This unique sign showed Mary, the sister of Henry VIII, who married Charles Brandon, Duke of Suffolk. She was obsessed by artichokes and simply could not eat enough of these vegetables.

Shoulder of Mutton. A fairly common sign, it usually shows a butcher chopping the joint. At one time, many publicans had a sideline in butchery to cater for hungry travellers. The Shoulder of Mutton and Cucumbers near Arundel in Sussex has a curious origin. Apparently the shoulder of mutton there was served with a cucumber sauce.

Sprat, Didcot, Oxfordshire. The sprat, a small member of the herring family, has long been prized as a cheap and tasty fish. Perhaps because it is usually deep-fried, which is regarded as an unhealthy way of cooking, it is no longer so much in demand. The fishing port of Brixham in Devon has, appropriately, a Sprat and Mackerel. The common expression 'to set a sprat to catch a mackerel' means to sacrifice something small in order to obtain something bigger and more worthwhile.

Sugar Loaf. This fairly uncommon sign is sometimes rendered in the plural. Until well into the nineteenth century, refined sugar was presented and retailed in the form of a distinctive cone. Grocers often used large models of the sugar loaf as a sign and so, on occasion, did publicans.

Yard of Ale. There are a few examples of this sign. The 'yard' is a specially made glass drinking vessel about a metre long with a bulb at one end. When full, it contains about 4 pints and it needs to be drained at a single draught, if the drinker wishes to avoid being doused in beer. Needless to say, few people can manage to do so, and few can keep that amount of beer swilling around in them without being sick.

Some Curious Names and Signs

Albion, Chester. This sign is redolent of patriotism. Albion is an ancient and poetic name for Britain, possibly from 'albus', the Latin for white and referring to the white cliffs of Dover. As so often happens, there are other explanations.

Ass in a Bandbox, near Knaresborough, North Yorkshire. The story is that during the reign of Queen Anne (reigned 1702–14), a bandbox was sent to a leading political figure. It contained three cocked and loaded pistols attached inside the lid and designed to go off when the box was opened. Fortunately the booby trap was discovered. The bandbox was then addressed to the person who had sent it but now inside the box were a pewter inkstand and some quill pens. The idea of these was to make an ass of the person who opened it when he realised that his evil plot had been foiled. During the wars with Napoleonic France in the early nineteenth century, the sign was repainted in a topical form. It showed an ass which was standing in a bandbox on the French coast. Astride the ass was a fuming Napoleon looking impotently out across the Channel to England.

Bell and Steelyard, Woodbridge, Suffolk. In this delightful old town stands a pub which was once called simply 'the Bell'. It had a steelyard jutting into the street, used as a crane for lifting purposes and left in place after it went out of use. This became such a familiar and loved relic that the pub was renamed in its honour.

Blind Jack's, Knaresborough, North Yorkshire. This is a newish pub with a congenially antique ambience. The name commemorates John Metcalf (1717–1810), nicknamed 'Blind Jack', who lost his sight in infancy but went on to become a fine athlete, horseman and, perhaps even more extraordinary, a successful road surveyor and engineer.

Bolt in Tun, London EC1. Our medieval ancestors were fond of the rebus or punning image. A Prior of St Bartholomew had the surname Bolton. While monks brewed ale as a matter of course, Bolton was acclaimed for the particularly good ale he produced when he took time off from his monastic duties. He was commemorated with a rebus. Arrows were often called 'bolts' and a 'tun' was a wine vessel; hence the pub commemorating the prior was the 'Bolt in Tun'.

Bombay Grab, London E3. A 'grab' was a kind of small two-masted sailing vessel that used to ply its trade along the coasts of India in the eighteenth and nineteenth centuries. Grabs ranged from about 150 to 300 tons. There is no explanation as to how one of these fairly ordinary little ships should bestow its name on a pub close to the River Thames and so far away from its home waters.

The Case is Altered. A small number of pubs bear this name, the origins of which are a matter for dispute among pub-sign aficionados. One version of the story is that a farmer kept a herd of cows which kept straying on to his neighbours' land and doing damage there. One of these neighbours, who fancied himself as a lawyer, threatened him by saying that if the animals strayed again the farmer would be liable for the cost of the damage they did. However, when the neighbour's own beasts got out and caused damage, he was completely silent because the boot was on the other foot – the case was altered. Another equally unlikely explanation concerns the publican of a disreputable house being threatened with the withdrawal of its licence unless he cleaned up his act. He did so and when he reapplied for his licence it was readily granted – hence the case is altered. More

bizarre is the claim that the pub got its name from an English corruption of 'Casa de Salter', a place in Spain where vigorous dancing took place.

Cow and Snuffers, Llandaff, Cardiff. This name is supposed to be the result of a challenge issued over two hundred years ago to see who could come up with a new name combining the two most incongruous elements.

Dewdrop Inn. This is an example of the genre of humorous punning pub names.

Dr Butler's Head, London EC2. This unique sign recalls a quack doctor or charlatan of the early seventeenth century who managed to insinuate himself into the affections of James I, who was a hypochondriac. Despite having no medical qualifications, 'Dr' Butler frequently attended the King. He also made a name for himself by inventing and marketing a popular 'medicinal' ale.

Fortune of War and Naked Boy, London EC1. The original name of this pub was the odd one of Naked Boy. The publican doubled as a tailor who under the appropriate sign had a little verse which went: 'So fickle is our English nation, I would be clothed if I knew the fashion.' The 'Fortune of War' part of the name came when a new landlord took the pub over. His previous pub went by that name as an ironic comment on the fact that as a seaman in the Royal Navy he had lost both legs and one arm in what proved to be the last sea battle in which he took part.

Grinning Rat, Ipswich. Not everyone likes modern names and signs but this one maintains an honourable tradition well.

Hermit of Redcoats, near Hitchin, Hertfordshire. Close to this pub lived a well-to-do recluse called James Lucas. His mother died in 1849 and he was struck down with a grief from which he never recovered. He simply withdrew into himself, barricaded the house against intruders and spent the rest of his life in the utmost filth and squalor. The only people he seemed pleased to see were tramps. If a 'gentleman of the road' turned up, Lucas would open a window and engage in animated conversation with him. The tramp would never leave empty-handed.

Jackson-Stops. This pub at Stretton in Rutland has a unique name. The pub went on the market under its previous name of White Horse with the firm of Jackson, Stops as the agent. Although it was still trading, it took years to sell. When a buyer was eventually found, the estate agent's sign had become so familiar that it was decided officially to rename the pub with what had become its popularly known nickname.

Labour in Vain. A few houses displayed this sign. It showed a white woman scrubbing a dark-skinned infant but obviously failing to get it 'clean'. It is likely that such signs have succumbed to political correctness.

March of Intellect, Hull. The story goes that this pub was once owned by two brothers who hired out their sons as climbing boys sweeping chimneys. The sign outside the pub showed two sweeps with the tools of their trade. Over time, the pub became known as 'the Sweeps' after its sign. At a later stage a wit added a further inscription under the sweeps. This was the laconic phrase 'the march of intellect', and before long that became first the nickname of the pub and then its official name. The pub is long gone.

Marlborough Arms, Chester. Spot the mistake. This is a fine example of a signwriter's inattention. The new name has become permanent.

Now Thus, Barton, Greater Manchester. The sign showed a man holding a flail, a manual tool used for threshing corn. It is said that the prominent local De Trafford family, who supported the Royalist cause during the English Civil War, were forewarned that their mansion was going to be raided by a force of Parliamentary troops. When the troops arrived, they searched high and low but could not find anything of value. Frustrated and angry, they went into an adjoining barn, where a yokel was busily threshing the corn. He appeared to be the village idiot because his only response to their questions was 'Now thus, now thus'. The soldiers went on their way, knowing they would get nothing out of him. The yokel was of course none other than De Trafford himself and under the straw that he had been threshing so vigorously were the family valuables. The De Traffords adopted as their crest a farmhand threshing with a flail and mouthing the words 'Now thus'.

Old Tippling Philosopher, Newport, South Wales. The name probably celebrates the Greek philosophers who liked to drink wine while engaged in the cut and thrust of their metaphysical argument.

Pot at Wot, Bristol. The sign shows a street urchin of the Victorian period putting a letter into an elegant pillar box of the same period. The full name of the pub is '*P*ost *O*ffice *T*avern at *W*estbury-*O*n-*T*rym'. The pub displays a lot of historical Post Office items.

Slip Inn, York. This punning sign shows a ship being launched.

Sun and Thirteen Cantons, London W1. Soho, where this pub is situated, is a part of London that used to attract foreign immigrants, often refugees, who settled and established businesses. Some became publicans and what was more natural than to give the pub a name and erect a sign that would attract their compatriots? A canton is a Swiss province and there was a sizeable Swiss population in the district.

Three Legs of Man. An unusual sign, this is mostly found in the north of England. It refers to the arms of the Isle of Man and shows three legs, the toes of which are pointing in different directions. Legend has it that the Isle of Man kneels to England, kicks at Scotland and spurns Ireland. One house with this name in Leeds had the nickname 'the Kettle with Three Spouts'.

Treaty of Commerce. This unique name adorns a pub in Lincoln. It recalls the 'Cobden Treaty' of 1860, steered through by Richard Cobden. It was a triumph for free trade, of which Cobden was an enthusiastic supporter. It allowed France to give favourable terms to British manufactured goods, in return for which Britain reduced duties on French wine, brandy and silks.

Tumble Down Dick. This rare sign recalls Richard Cromwell, who briefly held the office of Lord Protector after the death of his illustrious father, Oliver, in 1658. He was not a man of the same calibre as his father and would probably have preferred to live in obscurity. Despite a reputation for integrity, he was overwhelmed by financial and political problems and was overthrown in 1659. The nickname is not necessarily derisive.

Virginia Ash, Henstridge, Somerset. Sir Walter Raleigh is credited (or blamed) with having introduced the tobacco-smoking habit to England after one of his voyages to the North American colonies. Cigarettes were yet to be invented and tobacco was enjoyed in pipes, often of a cheap and disposable nature. The habit naturally raised some eyebrows at first and, with smoke emanating from his nose and mouth, it appeared as if the smoker was on fire. The sign showed Raleigh enjoying a puff and a servant hovering nearby ready to throw the contents of a bucket of water over him.

Widow's Son, London E3. Around the middle of the nineteenth century, the son of the landlady went off to sea. He promised his weeping mother that he would return by next Easter and she promised to have a hot cross bun ready for him. Sadly he never returned but the old lady, unwilling to believe that she would never see him again, faithfully baked a bun every year for the rest of her life. The buns were threaded through a string suspended from the ceiling and subsequent licensees have continued to add to the collection. Most of the buns were destroyed by enemy action but every year a detachment from the Royal Navy presents a new fresh one to the pub, whose alternative name is 'the Bun House'.

Some Miscellaneous Signs

SOME PUB names and signs do not readily lend themselves to being categorised. We have tried to provide some sense in these pages of the immense range of themes that they embrace and also of the variety of forms in which signs can appear. The following illustrations suggest how difficult some signs are to place.

Cat and Custard Pot. This rare sign celebrates a fictional pub of the same name in one of the amusing novels by Robert Surtees about fox-hunting.

Clifton, Bristol. This 'topographical' sign commemorates the nearby bridge across the Avon Gorge.

Cock and Bull, Cockermouth, Cumbria. This may commemorate the farmyard animals or celebrate the highly coloured and unbelievable tale known as a 'cock and bull' story.

Donkey and Buskins. This sign at Layer-de-la-Haye in Essex refers to the local legend that a farmer equipped his donkey with buskins which are leather leggings. The kind man was protecting the animal from the prickly gorse growing abundantly in the area.

Fox and Hounds, Chiswick, London W4. This pub has two names. One side of the building shows this name and sign. The other displays the Mawson Arms. The pub is adjacent to Fuller's brewery.

Globe, Newton St Loe, Somerset. This is a very attractive version of this sign but the inspiration is unknown.

Minster View, Howden, East Yorkshire. This topographical sign shows the huge parish church in what was once a significant medieval port.

Ring o' Bells, Bath. This is an unusual three-dimensional variant of a common sign.

Sun, Scarborough. This is an attractive modern version of a familiar sign.

Pub-sign Artists

THE WORLD of fine art looks down on pub signs but many great painters have cut their teeth in this genre, especially when they were setting out on their careers. Richard Wilson (1714–82) was a very fine landscape painter appreciated more overseas than in Britain during his lifetime, and it may have been lack of commissions of the sort he most wanted that led him to work on signboards. He died in poverty and may well have had to take any work that came his way.

George Morland (1763–1804) displayed precocious talent, encouraged by his father, who was also a painter. Morland is best-known for his paintings of alehouses, cottages and farmyards, which have a very English quality about them. Painting alehouses was a case of combining work with pleasure for Morland because he was a habitual drunkard who led a bohemian and dissipated lifestyle. Constantly broke, he spent time in prison for debt but was often known to knock off a painting in exchange for a meal and as much beer as he could drink.

The most eminent of the early pub-sign artists was William Hogarth (1697–1764). He was highly versatile but his best-known works are probably those which had a moral purpose and gave an insight into the mores of the time, such as *Beer Street* and *Gin Lane* of 1751. These constitute a forceful visual diatribe against the evils associated with the gin-drinking craze of the time. His best-known pub sign was the Man Loaded with Mischief, which at one time adorned an alehouse in what is now Oxford Street in London. The 'load of mischief' is the man's wife, to whom he is padlocked. She has a raven and a monkey as companions. Many copies and imitations of this sign are still in existence.

David Cox (1793–1859) was a painter of watercolours who did a fine sign for the Royal Oak at Betwys-y-Coed in North Wales; it is still on display, although now inside the building. John Berney Crome (1768–1821), known as 'Old Crome', took any job that came his way, among them being a sign for the Jolly Sailor at Great Yarmouth. More eminent were John Everett Millais (1829–96), who painted a sign for the George and Dragon at Hayes in Middlesex, and Walter Crane (1845–1915). He is thought of more as a designer and illustrator but he painted a sign for the Fox and Pelican at Grayshott in Hampshire.

In 1907 the *Illustrated London News* contained a feature depicting pub signs painted by Royal Academicians. Two of these showed the sign of the Miller of Mansfield at Goring, Oxfordshire, and were painted by Marcus Stone. Lady Elizabeth Georgiana painted the sign of the Ferry Inn at Rosneath in Scotland. The work of William Hogarth was represented by a sign for 'A Man with a Load of Mischief'. The original was possibly on a pub in Oxford Street, London but it was often reproduced and this one may have adorned a pub at Blewbury in Oxfordshire. This sign would now be politically incorrect because it showed a troubled man bearing a shrewish-looking woman and a monkey on his shoulders. Two well-known painters called Leslie and Hodson each painted one side of the George and Dragon signboard at Wargrave in Berkshire. It is said that they did the work in order to pay the substantial bill they had run up with the landlord.

Pub signs have always been a popular form of art and an exhibition of signboards was held in London in 1762. It was a spoof of the 'Exhibition of Polite Arts' organised annually by the Society of Manufactures, Arts and Commerce and was marketed as a 'poor man's art gallery'. The art profession was decidedly sniffy but the public loved it and the exhibition was a great success. In 1936 an Inn Signs Exhibition was held in the West End. There were over 250 actual signs plus a lot of pictorial and photographic material. The exhibition was open for four weeks, had almost eighteen thousand visitors and generated an enormous amount of interest. It opened the eyes of the public to the fact that inn signs were pieces of art offering scope not only for those who painted them but also in many cases for workers who created the necessary supportive wrought ironwork.

Many old signs were painted in oil straight on to a wooden surface. It is the nature of pub signs that they are exposed to weathering and dirt and these early signs did not prove very durable. Science has since come to the assistance of the sign-painter, who now often uses aluminium or special hard-wearing wood bases and also has available paints (often acrylics) and varnishes designed to withstand all that the elements can throw at them. For all that, signs do have a finite life. The irony of the sign-painter's work is that while it is seen by so many people it is unlikely that most of the observers take any time to examine the sign for more than a few seconds or even to give any thought as to who painted it. For all that, signs do have a finite life.

Few breweries now run sign-painting workshops although the St Austell Brewery in Cornwall and Wadworth's of Devizes are examples that do. The erstwhile brewers Whitbread had a workshop at Wateringbury in Kent for many years, with a team of artists who turned out many superb signs. This workshop later moved to another of the company's sites at Cheltenham before being closed in 1991. Since the mid-twentieth century some very high-quality artists have been at work. George Mackenney over a long career produced well over twelve thousand paintings. He researched his subjects thoroughly before beginning to work on the design and always liked to give the subject an alternative spin if that was possible. He also felt that it was always important to present a sign that was historically accurate. Stanley Chew was another prolific inn-sign artist with a wealth of fine signs to his credit. Pub-sign painters are still at work and can be contacted via the internet. While some signs exhibit poor artwork and a lack of craftsmanship or inadequate research, at their best, pub signs can be magnificent examples of a specialized artistic genre. The pub sign painter is producing an advertisement for the premises involved. He needs to create something eye-catching which either immediately conveys its meaning or is a subtle or humorous allusion to the name of the pub. Since so many pub names provide historical insights, a working knowledge which includes the byways of history is also a distinct advantage.

Many social history and folk museums have one or two signboards on display. The two largest collections available for public viewing are those at the Castle Museum in York and the Museum of London, London Wall, EC2. The first of these has re-creations of streets, courts and alleys; among businesses included are pubs and there are at least five pub signs. The Museum of London has a number of signs from erstwhile pubs in the City of London, several of which are carved in stone. They include a massive sign which once adorned the outside of an inn with the very strange name of the Bull and Mouth. Some people think that this refers to a naval skirmish with the French during the reign of Henry VIII (1509–47). This took place at the entrance, or mouth, to the harbour at Boulogne and 'Bull and Mouth' is said to be a corruption by English people whose French pronunciation was none too good.

Another fascinating sign is the three-dimensional Goose & Gridiron. The two elements in this name seem totally disparate unless you know that this is actually a religious sign. The leading saints all had symbols in religious iconography and the goose and the gridiron both symbolized St Laurence. Now for the nasty bit. Laurence was a Roman who died in AD 258. It was his ill luck to be a professing Christian at a time when they were suffering severe persecution. The story is that he was martyred for his beliefs by being roasted on a gridiron, this accounting for the second of the two symbols by which he was known. The story of the roasting is entirely apocryphal. Laurence did indeed suffer a martyr's death but the Roman authorities beheaded him, which was what they did with such troublesome people.

There are some signs in the Victoria and Albert Museum in London, and a trip to the Coors Brewery Visitor Centre in Burton upon Trent for their material on the history and art of inn signs will be rewarding.

Pubs with Nicknames

By any criteria, pubs and other drinking places have played an enormous part in the social, political and cultural history of Britain. Although there has always been an often vociferous minority hostile to the consumption of alcohol, far larger numbers have held pubs, the products they sell and the ambience they provide in very high regard. We have already seen just how diverse is the range of the official names of pubs but because of their importance in the life of the community, or for some other concrete reason, they have often been given nicknames. These nicknames are equally diverse and fascinating. Here we provide some examples from Liverpool, chosen because of the author's familiarity with the district and because these names reflect the robust local humour. Many of these pubs are no longer trading but the nicknames hint at the crucial role they played in the community. Listed under districts of the city, the pub's official name is given first and then the everyday name.

North Liverpool

Waterloo Hotel – *Geraghty's Vaults*; Convivial – *Poison 'Arry's*; Globe Boathouse – *Broken Nosed Jack's*; Coach and Horses – *Wynne's*; Jamaica – *The Rat*; Knowsley Arms – *Blue House*; Grapes Hotel – *Smokin' Joe's*; Queen's Arms – *Bath House*; Sefton Arms – *Banjo Bennett's*; Barlow Hotel – *Dark House*; Prince of Wales – *Sod House*; Catherine Hotel – *Salt Box*.

North-east Liverpool

Crown Inn – *Tom Snuff's*; Morning Star – *Blood's*; Britannia – *Mary Kate's*; Bevington Arms – *Sweat Rag*; Brewery Vaults – *Bean House*; Halfway House – *Fitzy's*; Canterbury Arms – *Fish House*; Market Inn – *Woodbines*; Tatlock Vaults – *Effin' Nellie's*; Audley Arms – *Joe's*; Grapes – *Mad Dan's*; Rock Light – *May's*; Swan Vaults – *Gertie's*; Peacock – *The Anderson.*

South and east Liverpool

Brunswick Hotel – *Seven Steps*; Alexandra – *Mad House*; Clevedon Arms – *Glue Pot*; Coburg Hotel – *Devil's*; Prince's Park Hotel – *Sadie's*; Grecian – *Snake Pit*; Royal George – *Black's*; Warwick Castle – *Rat*; Wellington Vaults – *Charley Fay's*; Windsor Hotel – *The Clock*; Spekeland – *Joney's*; New Pavilion – *Macaulay's*; Newstead Abbey – *Irish House.*

Sometimes a pub's nickname becomes its official name. A good example is the Grapes in Egerton Street, Liverpool 8, which came to be known as 'Peter Kavanagh's' after a well-known licensee, who was also a prominent city councillor. Although the future of the pub is uncertain, it is still known to all and sundry as 'Peter Kavanagh's'. Another example is the former Mount at Dingle, which is now 'Sixy's' – this was its previous nickname, gained because for a long time it had only a six-day licence, not opening on a Sunday. The reason for a pub's common name is often lost. The most common themes seem to be some distinctive physical feature of the building or its neighbourhood or the name of a particular, perhaps long-standing licensee, or occasionally some characteristic that marked him or her out.

Further Reading

There is a dearth of books on pub signs, given the intrinsic interest of the subject. Many of those listed below are not in print but may be found in second-hand bookshops and via the internet.

Corballis, Paul. *Pub Signs.* Headline, 1988.

Cox, Barrie. *English Inn and Tavern Names.* English Place-Name Society, 1994.

Delderfield, Eric R. *British Inn Signs and Their Stories.* David & Charles, 1965

Delderfield, Eric R. *Inns and Their Signs.* 1975.

Delderfield, Eric R. *Introduction to Pub Signs.* 1969.

Delderfield, Eric R. *Stories of Inns and Their Signs.* David & Charles, 1974.

Dunkling, Leslie, and Wright, Gordon. *A Dictionary of Pub Names.* Routledge & Kegan Paul, 1987.

Jack, Albert. *The Old Dog and Duck.* Particular Books, 2009.

Larwood, James, and Hotten, J. C. *English Inn Signs.* Chatto & Windus, revised edition 1951.

Rotheroe, Dominic. *London Inn Signs.* Shire, 1990.

Saunders, E. *A Book about Pub Names.* 2008.

Thorne, J. *A Bibliophile's Inn-signia.* 1997.

Waters, Colin. *A Dictionary of Pub, Inn and Tavern Signs.* Countryside Books, 2005.

Whitbread & Co. *Inn-signia.* Whitbread, 1948.

Wright, G. *At the Sign of the Flagon.* 1970.

The Inn Sign Society brings together those interested in researching, recording and sharing knowledge about the origins, history and meaning of pub signs in Britain and abroad. The Society publishes an excellent illustrated journal for members called *At the Sign of...* The contact is Mr Alan Rose, 9 Denmead Drive, Wednesfield, Wolverhampton WV11 2QS. Information is available at info@the innsignsociety.com

Index

Albion 62
Aleppo Merchant 23
Ale-stake 5
Alexandra Vaults 16
Alice Hawthorne 20
Altisidora 20
Angel 8, *8*
Anne of Cleves 16
Apollo 50
Ark Royal 23
Artizan 56
Atmospheric Railway 34

Badger Hounds 27, *27*
Banker 56
Baron of Beef 59
Barrow Boy and Banker 56
Baseball Tavern 27
Bass House 59
Bear 42, *42*
Bear & Billet and variations 16–17
Beehive 46
Bell, 23, *23*
Bell and Steelyard 62
Bendigo 28
Betsey Trotwood 53, *53*
Bilbo Baggins 53
Bird in Hand 28, *28*
Black Beauty 54
Bladud's Head 50
Blake, Admiral 38
Bleeding Wolf 42–3
Blind Jack's 62–3
Blue Boar 17
Bolt in Tun 63
Bombay Grab 63
Bowlturners Arms 56
Bramley Apple 59
Brass Monkey 23
Brewer and Firkin 56
Brigadier Gerard 20
Brunel Arms 34–5
Buck 43
Bull 8, 43, *43*
Bull and Mouth 72–3
Byron, Lord 32, *32*

Cadland, 20
Café Royal 59–60
Cardigan, Earl of 39
Cartoonist 31
Case is Altered 63, *63*
Castle Museum, York 72
Cat 43
Cat & Custard Pot 68, *68*
Catherine Wheel 8–9
Cavendish Arms 17, *17*
Charles XII 21
Cheshire Cheese 60
Christopher 9
Churchill Arms 39
Clifton 68, *68*
Coach & Horses 12
Cobbett, William 33
Cock 46–7
Cock and Bull 68
Cock & Pye 9
Cordwainers Arms 17
Cow and Snuffers 63
Cox, David 71
Crab 47
Crab & Winkle 34
Crane 47, *47*
Crane, Walter 71
Cross Keys 9, *9*
Crutched Friars 10, *10*
Cuckoo Bush 50–1
Cumberland 17, *17*

Dairy Maid 12
Dewdrop 64
Dickens, Charles 31
Dog 43–4
Dog and Duck 28
Dolphin 47
Donkey & Buskins 68, *68*
Dove 47
Dr Butler's Head 64
Drovers' Arms 12
Dun Cow 44

Eagle and Child 17
Earl of Cardigan 39
Elephant 44
Ellis, William Webb 29
Endeavour 24
Engineers' Arms 57
EUR 35, *35*
Evening Star 35

Falmouth Packet 24
Ferry 71
Fighting Cocks 28
Five Bells 24
Fitzwilliam Arms 17
Fleece 57
Fleming, Sir Alexander 41, *41*
Flying Childers 21, *21*
Flying Dutchman 21
Fortune of War and

Naked Boy 64
Four Marys, 17
Fox 44, *44*
Fox and Hounds 28, 68
Framesmiths' Arms 57
Frying Pan 60

Gainsborough 31
Gallows Signs 6
George, Stamford, Lincs 6
George & Dragon 9
George & Pilgrims, Glastonbury 9–10
Gilbert and Sullivan 31
Globe 69, *69*
Gluepot 35
Goat & Compasses 69 *69*
Golden Cross 10
Golden Fleece 51, *51*
Golden Lion 18
Goose 47–8
Goose and Cuckoo 48
Goose and Gridiron 73
Granby, Marquis of 40–1, *40–1*
Grand Junction Arms 24, *24*
Great Eastern 24
Great Western 35, *35*
Greengage 60
Green Man 51, *51*
Grinning Rat 64, *64*
Guide over Sands 12
Gunners 28

Hackney Cab 13
Hand & Flowers 64, *64*
Hansom Cab 13, *13*
Hark to Mopsey 28
Havelock, General 40
Hermit of Redcoats 64, *64*
Hero of Aliwal 40, *40*
Hitchcock, Sir Alfred 32
Hogarth, William 70–1
Hope 24–5
Hope & Anchor 10, *10*
Horse and Jockey and variations 21
Hurdler 28

Iron Devil 48

Jackson-Stops 64–5, *64–5*
Jekyll and Hyde 54
Jet Miners 57
John, Augustus 30
John Barleycorn 51
Jolly Buffer 57, *57*
Jolly Colliers 57
Jolly Roger 25
Jones, John Paul 40, *40*
Jonson, Ben 30–1

Kavanagh's, Peter 75, *75*
King Arthur 51
King Lud 51
King's Head 18, *18*

Labour in Vain 65
Lamb and Flag 10
Lamplighters 57–8
Larwood and Voce 29
Lattice House, 5
Laurel and Hardy 31–2
Light Railway 36
Lion 44–5
Llandoger Trow 25
Lock, Stock & Barrel 13
Locomotive 37
London, Museum of 72–3
Lorna Doon 54

Macaulay Arms 32
Mackenney, George 72
Maiden Over 29
Man with a Load of Mischief 71
Mannering, Captain 38
March of Intellect 65
Marlborough Arms 65, *65*
Marvell, Andrew 30
Master Robert 21
Midget 13
Midland Railway 36
Millais, John Everett 71
Miller of Mansfield 71
Minster View 69, *69*
Morland, George 70
Museum of London 72–3

Navigation 13
Now Thus 65

Oakeley Arms 18, *18*
Old Blue Anchor Stores 25, *25*
Old Crome 32, 71
Old Tippling Philosophers 66
Orange Tree 60, *60*

Ox 46
Oxnoble 60

Packhorse 13
Packhorse & Talbot 13, *13*
Parrot 48
Peregrine 48
Perseverance 12
Pigeon Pie 60–1
Pike 48
Plimsoll Arms 25
Plum Tree 61
Pot at Wot 66
Pride of Paddington 36
Princess of Wales 18

Queen's Head and Artichoke 61

Racecourse 21
Railway 36
Railway Swan 36–7
Ramsay, Allan 30
Red Lion 18, *18*
Richard II, King 5
Ring O' Bells 69
Rising Sun 18, *18*
Robin Hood 52 *52*
Robinson Crusoe 54
Robinson, Leefe 40
Royal Oak 18–19
Royal Sovereign 26
Running Footman 14, *14*

St Austell Brewery 72
St John's Head 10–11
St Leger 21
Salutation 11
Saracen's Head 11
Scotsman's Pack 14
Scott, Sir Walter 33
Sea Horse 48–9, *48–9*
Seven Stars 11, *11*
Sherlock Holmes 54–5, *54–5*
Ship 26
Ship and Trades 58
Shoulder of Mutton 61
Shroppie Fly 14
Silent Whistle 37
Silver Jubilee 37
Sixy's 75
Sky Blue 29
Slip Inn 66, *66*
Slubbers Arms 19
Sole Bay Inn 69
Spinner and Bergamot 21–2
Sprat 61
Spyglass & Kettle 37
Squinting Cat 45
Stable Door 22
Stanley, Chew 72
Starting Gate 22
Steelmelters' Arms 58
Stephenson, George 35
Straw Bear 52
Sugar Loaf 61
Sun 69
Sun and Thirteen Cantons 66
Surtees 33
Swan 49

Tabernae 4–5
Talbot 19
Tattersall's Tavern 22
Three Compasses 58, *58*
Three Kings 11
Three Legs of Man 66
Three Men in a Boat 55
Tollgate 14
Tramways 14–15
Travellers Rest 15
Treaty of Commerce 66
Tumble Down Dick 66–7
Turbinia 26
Turpin's Cave 52

Unicorn 19

Van Tromp 41
Victoria 19
Virginia Ash 67

Wadworth's Brewery 72
Waggon and Horses 15
Warren, Sir John Borlase, 41
Wellington, Duke of 39,*39*
Wheeltappers 58
White Hart, Scole, Norfolk 6
White Horse 19
White Lion 19
Whitesmiths' Arms 58
Why Not? 22
Widow's Son 67
Wilson, Richard 70
Wolseley, Sir Garnet 41

Yard of Ale 61
Ye Olde Starre, York 6
Ye Olde Trip to Jerusalem, Nottingham 4
Yorker 29